—— THE WRITING OF ELENA PONIATOWSKA ——

ELENA PONIATOWSKA
PHOTO BY GIGI KAESER

The Texas Pan American Series

THE WRITING OF ELENA PONIATOWSKA

Engaging Dialogues

BETH E. JÖRGENSEN

UNIVERSITY OF TEXAS PRESS
AUSTIN

Requests for permission to reproduce material from this work
should be sent to Permissions, University of Texas Press, Box
7819, Austin, TX 78713-7819.

∞ The paper used in this publication meets the minimum
requirements of American National Standard for Information
Sciences—Permanence of Paper for Printed Library Materials,
ANSI Z39.48−1984.

LIBRARY OF CONGRESS CATALOGING-IN-
PUBLICATION DATA
Jörgensen, Beth Ellen.
The writing of Elena Poniatowska : engaging dialogues / Beth E.
Jörgensen. — 1st ed.
p.   cm.
Includes bibliographical references (p.   ) and index.
ISBN 0-292-74032-8 (alk. paper). — ISBN 0-292-74033-6 (pbk.)
1. Poniatowska, Elena—Criticism and interpretation. I. Title
PQ7297.P63Z73   1994
868—dc20   93-37776

For Dorothy and Charles Jörgensen,
Tom Covell, and Megan and
Benjamin Jörgensen Covell.

CONTENTS

ACKNOWLEDGMENTS

My interest in the writing of Elena Poniatowska began when I was a graduate student working with Professor Zunilda Gertel. My first expression of thanks goes to her for many years of intellectual exchange and personal encouragement.

This project has taught me much about the pleasures of building friendships through a shared passion for reading and writing. A dozen years ago Elena Poniatowska responded to a phone call from an unknown graduate student with a graciousness and generosity that I now know are deeply ingrained habits of the heart. For her hospitality in Mexico City, her interest in my work, her unfailing courtesy, and our many conversations together, I am most grateful. I am equally grateful to Irene Matthews, who has played an invaluable role in the writing and rewriting of this manuscript. I owe an enormous debt to her careful, critical reading of all four chapters, her practical advice on a myriad of mundane concerns, and the strong support of her friendship at every step of the way toward publication of the book.

This project, like all research, has benefited from the contributions of many other individuals as well, and I would like to recognize those who have been most directly involved. My colleagues Robert Blake, Gerald Bond, and Claudia Schaefer read and commented on early versions of the introduction and chapters 2 and 3. Through our common enthusiasm for Mexico and

Elena's writing both Doris Meyer and Nina M. Scott have become valued mentors and friends in the course of writing this book. Carolyn Malloy and Rafael Madrid were my hosts on my first visit to Mexico in 1982, and I continue to count on their expertise and knowledge in many ways. A faculty leave granted by the University of Rochester in the spring of 1991 enabled me to finish a substantial portion of the manuscript.

Finally, I want to thank a woman who enjoys a well-deserved reputation among Latin Americanists as the very best of editors, Theresa May of the University of Texas Press. She and the other editors who worked on this manuscript, Carolyn Wylie and Mary Hill, made the whole publication process an exciting and rewarding experience.

Permission to use portions of previously copyrighted material was generously granted by *Hispanic Journal, Latin American Perspectives*, and *Texto Crítico*.

INTRODUCTION
"Engaging Dialogues"

"One of the defining qualities of your writing is the imprint of other voices on the page. You have a tremendous capacity for engaging people in dialogue— even, or perhaps especially, people with whom you seem to have little in common."

"I think it comes very naturally to me. I just have a way of making people want to talk about themselves, and I have never in my life felt any rejection out on the street, from the people. I'd say it has a lot to do with my foreignness, with my desire to belong. It also has a great deal to do with the fact that I didn't learn Spanish from my family, but rather with the people who worked in our home. That created an initial closeness, and later I've always been able to speak easily with everyone. Colloquial language is a bond between us, and people respond easily to me."

"Isn't dialogue also a way of knowing yourself and of creating yourself, or of creating a personal identity?"
"I think so, although I don't have a very clear idea of myself . . . It has always been difficult for me to personalize things, and moreover it doesn't even interest me. I'm always more interested in the other." [1]

BIOGRAPHY

In her forty-year career as a journalist, novelist, short story writer, and essayist, Elena Poniatowska has earned wide recognition as one of contemporary Latin America's most original and productive authors. Some of her texts chronicle such collective, public events as the 1968 Mexican student movement, a hunger strike by mothers of the "disappeared," and the 1985 earthquake in Mexico City, while others reconstruct individual life stories in biographical, testimonial, and epistolary form. In all cases, Poniatowska's work offers a critical—and self-critical—perspective on contemporary Mexican reality by recuperating previously silenced versions of events and by scrutinizing her own considerable stake in the status quo.

Elena Poniatowska's journalistic specialty is the interview, a genre that she has transformed within Mexico, and much of her writing bears the trace of her conversations with members of all sectors of Mexican society. The titles of her best-known books, *Hasta no verte Jesús mío, La noche de Tlatelolco, De noche vienes*, and *Fuerte es el silencio*, evoke for her readers the major themes and the diverse literary languages which her work embraces. Never bound by an adherence to established genres, Poniatowska frequently creates hybrid texts by combining the discourses of fact and fiction and by utilizing many linguistic registers and literary forms. These formal innovations correspond to the exigencies of her investigation into class, gender, and ethnic difference, the struggle of women and the poor for economic and social justice, and the mechanisms of repression of that struggle. Elena Poniatowska follows a long and well-documented tradition in Latin America of socially committed writers emerging from among the elite classes. Recently much attention has also been given to the attempts by subaltern people to record their experiences with as little interference from "above" as possible. Poniatowska occupies a curious and ambiguous position with regard to both tendencies, and in my study of selected works by the Mexican writer I show how her investment in dialogue creates the conditions for producing contestatory narratives in a variety of forms.

Elena Poniatowska Amor was born in Paris, France, in 1932. Her father, Juan Evremont Poniatowski Sperry, was a Frenchman of Polish origin who traced his ancestry back to King Stanislaus II, the last king of Poland before the 1795 partition.[2] Her mother is Paula Amor de Poniatowski, the French-born daughter of wealthy Mexican landowners who lost their rural holdings, but not their capital, during the agrarian reforms of the Lázaro Cárdenas administration (1934–1940). Elena and her younger sister, Kitzia, were raised in France, where they attended the first few years of primary school. While their parents took part in the French war effort, the two girls lived with their grandparents in the relative safety of the countryside in the south of France. In 1942 Paula Amor took her daughters to Mexico to escape wartime hostilities and deprivations. Elena Poniatowska has said that because of their many separations during her early years, she first discovered her mother, and her mother's Mexican nationality, on the voyage to her new homeland.

Once in Mexico City, Paula Amor de Poniatowski and her daughters settled into the home of the girls' maternal grandmother, and Elena and Kitzia were sent to a private British-run academy called the Windsor School. Later they attended the Liceo Franco-Americano in Mexico City, and Elena Poniatowska finished high school with two years in the United States at the Sacred Heart Convent near Philadelphia, Pennsylvania. The future writer's finishing school education emphasized the necessary lessons for a wealthy Catholic girl destined for marriage and raising a family: training in piano and voice, ballroom dancing, etiquette, sewing, foreign languages, a smattering of literature and composition, and a heavy dose of Bible study and Catholic doctrine. Constrained by finances from going on to college in the United States, she found herself at age eighteen back in Mexico City without any clear plans for her future and without any useful professional credentials. Ruling out an early marriage as well as a European tour, she was encouraged to become a trilingual secretary, and she dabbled at classes in stenography without any great success.

The details of Elena Poniatowska's privileged, European-oriented upbringing do not predict her present stature as a major chronicler of recent Mexican history and culture. Moreover, Poniatowska denies having felt a strong vocation for writing as a child, and she adds that she never made a conscious decision to pursue a career as a writer. The mother of three grown children, Elena Poniatowska was married to the Mexican astronomer Guillermo Haro, who died in 1988. Although she occasionally alludes to the many tensions caused by deliberately combining family and work responsibilities, like many other women of high achievement she usually chooses to emphasize the serendipitous nature of her professional life. As Poniatowska tells it, in 1954 she chanced upon an opportunity to interview the new ambassador to Mexico from the United States. She took the interview to a family friend at the daily newspaper *Excélsior*, then a pro-American publication, and was given a job doing interviews and writing up society news. She remained at *Excélsior* for one year and conducted an interview per day with writers, artists, musicians, and other cultural and political figures. In 1955 she moved to another Mexico City daily, *Novedades*, for which she has continued to write up to the present, at first very steadily and now more sporadically. Thus, despite the classic feminine protestations that her career simply happened to her, Elena Poniatowska has long lived out a deliberate and even defiant dedication to the writer's life.

Elena Poniatowska's cultivation of the journalistic interview opened up new worlds of thought and action for the young reporter, and over the years her work as a journalist and her own reading have more than compensated for the deficiencies of her early intellectual training. She, in turn, brought a fresh, somewhat irreverent approach to the extremely formal journalistic style current among her more established and virtually all male colleagues in the 1950s press. In chapter 1 of this study I look closely at her early method of interviewing and at how the resulting articles pay tribute to the prevailing social and gender hierarchy, while also posing a limited challenge to the authority of her prominent interviewees.

Besides her work for *Novedades*, Elena Poniatowska has contributed articles and interviews over the years to most of Mexico's principal journals and newspapers, including *Siempre!*,

Vuelta, and *Plural*. Since late 1985, when *Novedades* refused to publish her daily articles about the devastating September 19 earthquake in Mexico City, Poniatowska has collaborated actively with *La Jornada*, a leftist newspaper which picked up the earthquake series when *Novedades* dropped it. Poniatowska was a founding editor in 1976 of *fem*, Mexico's longest surviving feminist magazine, for which she has also written numerous essays. Elena Poniatowska distinguishes herself by her feminist stance in a country where intellectual women have frequently taken pains to disassociate themselves from feminism. Other significant contributions to Mexican intellectual and artistic life include a role in founding the Cineteca Nacional (a national film library) and her part in the 1967 birth of Editorial Siglo Veintiuno, now an important press with affiliates in Spain, Colombia, and Argentina. In 1978 she was awarded the National Journalism Prize for the interview genre, the first woman ever to receive that honor.

Elena Poniatowska's great success as a writer has translated into opportunities to teach inside and outside Mexico. For many years now she has led a weekly writers' workshop in the suburb of Tlacopac. There she reads the works-in-progress of the group's twenty-five or so participants, and she facilitates the discussion of their projects. A number of novels have been published by members of that workshop, including *La mañana debe seguir gris* by Silvia Molina and *Novia que te veas* by Rosa Nissan. This group also worked closely with her on the gathering and editing of the earthquake testimonies. In 1979 the University of Sinaloa granted Elena Poniatowska an honorary doctorate of humane letters, and she has received numerous other academic honors over the last decade. Poniatowska has held visiting professorships at the University of California, Davis (fall 1987), and at the Five Colleges in Massachusetts (fall 1991). She has also served as a regents' lecturer in the University of California system. She speaks frequently in Mexico, the United States, and Europe and increasingly throughout Latin America.

No one could deny that Elena Poniatowska has drawn incalculable professional benefits from the practice of journalism. Economic independence, contact with other writers, the discipline of deadlines and collaborative work, and privileged access to persons and events and the institutional authority to speak about them have been decisive factors in her formation as a writer. Yet she has, for her part, contributed even more than she has gained. Her method of investigative interviewing and reporting and her dedication to recuperating marginalized perspectives on the national life have highly influenced younger writers. Remarkably, at the same time that she has made a major impact on Mexican journalism, Elena Poniatowska has established herself as an outstanding novelist and short story writer. Journalism and imaginative literature have always been simultaneous and intertwined activities in Poniatowska's professional life, and her extensive bibliography contains ground-breaking works of both fiction and nonfiction.

An overview of Elena Poniatowska's published books shows how the traditional boundaries between journalistic and literary modes of writing blur in her production, as they have tended to blur in the writings of her contemporaries inside and outside Mexico. *Lilus Kikus* (1954) is Poniatowska's first published title. It is a series of twelve brief, semi-autobiographical narratives about an upper-middle-class girl growing up in Mexico City. Poniatowska next published a satirical play, her sole attempt at drama, about Mexican intellectuals, *Melés y Teleo* (1956), in the journal *Panoramas*. *Palabras cruzadas* (1961, Crossed words) is an anthology of her early interviews selected from ones previously published in *Excélsior* and *Novedades*. *Todo empezó el domingo* (1963, It all began on Sunday), a group of short *costumbrista* pieces, represents the author's first efforts to document the experiences of the urban lower classes. *Los cuentos de Lilus Kikus* (1967, The Lilus Kikus stories) and *De noche vienes* (1979, The night visitor) are short story collections.

With the publication of *Hasta no verte Jesús mío* (Here's looking at you, Jesus) in 1969, Elena Poniatowska achieved increasing notoriety and a greatly expanded reading public in Mexico and abroad. Based in part on the testimony of an elderly laundrywoman whom Poniatowska met in the early 1960s, this novel has sparked an ongoing debate over the status of authorship and referentiality in a literary text which blends the docu-

mentary and the fictional into a seamless narrative. Elena Poniatowska won the 1970 Premio Mazatlán de Literatura for *Hasta
no verte Jesús mío*. As an interesting aside, newspaper articles
announcing the Mazatlán prize drop tantalizing hints that her
selection was a controversial one. *Excélsior* of March 16, 1971,
reports that a reception at Bellas Artes and a cocktail party were
scheduled to celebrate the event but then abruptly canceled; and
the amount of the monetary award, usually 25,000 pesos, was
mysteriously reduced to 15,000.

Beginning with the publication of *La noche de Tlatelolco*
(1971; *Massacre in Mexico*, 1975), the last twenty years have
witnessed enormous and diverse activity on the author's part,
activity which shows no signs of letting up. The common thread
that connects her varied works—political and social chronicles,
novels, short stories, interviews, and testimonies—is the author's
commitment to interpreting contemporary society. In particular,
Elena Poniatowska pays careful attention to the silenced voices
and the marginalized lives that constitute the disenfranchised
majority in the vast human landscape of Mexico. *La noche de
Tlatelolco* documents the 1968 Mexican student movement, using both oral history and contemporary written accounts of the
events of July to December 1968 to reconstruct a story which
the Mexican government had actively suppressed. The epistolary novel *Querido Diego, te abraza Quiela* (1976; *Dear Diego*,
1986) recreates a nine-month period in the life of Russian painter
Angelina Beloff, who lived with Diego Rivera in Paris until his
return to Mexico in 1921. *Gaby Brimmer* (1979), co-authored
with the book's protagonist, is a testimonial account of the life
of a young quadriplegic woman. *Fuerte es el silencio* (1980,
Strong is silence) collects four chronicles of recent events in Mexico, including a hunger strike by mothers of disappeared persons
and the enormous migration from the countryside to the Mexican capital. *Domingo siete* (1982, Seven on Sunday) is com-
prised of interviews with the seven candidates for president of
Mexico in the July 1982 elections.

In the 1980s, Elena Poniatowska collaborated on a number of
photographic essays for which she provided the written text. Examples are *La casa en la tierra* (1980, The house on the land),

with photos by Mariana Yampolsky; *El último guajolote* (1982, The last turkey), using archival photos of street vendors and traditional artisans of Mexico City; and *Las mujeres de Juchitán* (1989, The women of Juchitán), with photos by Graciela Iturbide. She has also written prologues to books that feature individual photographers, and she has just completed a long biographical novel on Tina Modotti, the Italian photographer who came to Mexico in the 1920s with Edward Weston. Poniatowska's fascination with photography stems from her experience as a journalist. She has worked closely with leading Mexican photographers and, early in her career, she did her own photography on some assignments. For Elena Poniatowska, photography, like print journalism, is both a documentary and a creative art with a unique power to interpret the world around us.

Five additional titles bring her bibliography up to date. In the essays of *¡Ay vida, no me mereces!* (1986, Life, you don't deserve me!) Elena Poniatowska pays tribute to contemporary Mexican authors who have had a strong impact on her career: Rosario Castellanos, Juan Rulfo, Carlos Fuentes and the writers of La Onda, José Agustín, Parménides García Saldaña, and Gustavo Sáinz. *La "Flor de Lis"* (1988, Fleur de lis) narrates the childhood and coming of age of a wealthy girl in the 1940s and early 1950s in Mexico City. *Nada, nadie: Las voces del temblor* (Nothing, nobody: Voices from the earthquake), also published in 1988, is a collage of testimonies about the 1985 earthquake in Mexico City. These two books, published in the same year, perfectly exemplify the writer's capacity for innovation in fictional and in documentary discourses. Since then, Poniatowska has been at work on a projected series of twelve volumes of her interviews, the first of which, *Todo México I* (All of Mexico I), appeared in 1990. Finally, more than a decade of research and writing culminated in the publication in 1992 of *Tinísima*, the biographical novel about Tina Modotti. With *Tinísima* Elena Poniatowska won the prestigious Mazatlán literary prize for the second time.

Even such a rapidly drawn and incomplete sketch of Elena Poniatowska's career and her published titles portrays the author as a deeply engaged chronicler of her nation's life who moves among an astonishingly broad cross-section of Mexican society.

The story of her writing is, thus, the story of her encounter with Mexico, and her texts inscribe the ever-changing relationship between her voice and the voices of her diverse compatriots. Certainly, the unique quality of Elena Poniatowska's writing, the quality celebrated in the title of my book, is dialogue: the dialogue that she has actively sought, first from a position as a cultural outsider, and then from a position of increased cultural rootedness and authority within Mexico. The dynamics of reciprocity and mutual influence between speakers in a conversation make it an ideal forum for the exploration of self and of other which is central to Poniatowska's work. On another level, she encourages a dialogue between conventionally distinct modes of writing by connecting the practices of journalism and imaginative literature in her work. As a point of departure, then, the exchange which I quoted at the beginning of this introduction sets out the terms of my analysis of selected works by Elena Poniatowska: an examination of how dialogue, understood as the site of encounter between different spoken languages and different speaking subjects, structures the process of production, the configuration of the text, and the reading of that text.

"CROSSED WORDS"

Dialogue and subjectivity: these two words continually cross paths in the present study. Each term alone already signifies a crossing of verbal paths. A dialogue is a linguistic bridge across the silent space of difference and ignorance. Subjectivity is located in the intersection of languages that construct the positions which we temporarily occupy and from which we speak. Dialogue and subjectivity are thus, indeed, doubly crossed words, *palabras cruzadas*; a puzzling crossword that presents ambiguous clues and an ever-shifting configuration of blanks. How wonderfully appropriate that the title of Elena Poniatowska's own first book of interviews generously offers the figure of speech which we may now turn to our advantage as an instrument of interpretation. *Palabras cruzadas*: an exchange of words between two speakers which, with a slight twist of the tongue, bespeaks an exchange of worlds. Another tiny turn and we cross swords, our tongues not only a bridge to knowledge, but also blades engaged in a duel for discursive authority. Whether as an act of communication or confrontation, Elena Poniatowska's writing represents a version of that play of voice and silence, speech and listening which constructs self and other in the space where our words cross.

To use the word "dialogue" in literary studies today necessarily invokes the work of Russian theorist Mikhail Bakhtin. Bakhtin himself asserted that any word is always already half someone else's and not an empty signifier at our individual command. In like fashion, his formulation of the concept of dialogism to explain the specificity of novelistic discourse and the authority of his usage of the term populate my references to dialogue in the writing of Elena Poniatowska. The primacy of speech and the incorporation of heterogeneous languages in her testimonial works—languages which she has mediated but not entirely subsumed under her own voice—are just the most visible manifestations of the kind of textual polyphony that characterizes such books as *Hasta no verte Jesús mío* and *La noche de Tlatelolco*. Further, Bakhtin's insights into how individual positionality and perception "must clothe themselves in the word, become utterances" are fundamental to my analysis of the tension in Elena Poniatowska's writing between social chronicle and self-inscription.[3] In this regard, I pay close attention to the ways in which "voices collide" on the pages of her texts. As Bakhtin points out, this collision of voices occurs between the utterances of different speakers and between words within an individual utterance.[4] The critical and self-critical potential of the novel, its status as a flexible genre-in-the-making, its emphasis on the present, and its special relationship with extraliterary genres (letters, diary, journalism) are other attributes ascribed by Bakhtin to the novel and which elucidate Elena Poniatowska's literary production. Finally, the recognition that discourse is always a social phenomenon and that a given text, like the world itself, is internally contradictory and multilanguaged operates throughout my study.

Mikhail Bakhtin places the rise of the modern European polyphonic novel in the context of a complex and centuries-long struggle of cultures. He looks beyond isolated "national" traditions to plot historical trends in literary production and reception across political boundaries. The influential phenomena which he identifies include all manner of translations of works from one language to another, the development of the printing press, and the increasing contact between cultures across ethnic and linguistic lines. All these factors heighten a writer's awareness of the plurality of social languages and competing systems of thought. Elena Poniatowska has personally lived out the kind of "verbal and semantic decentering" that Bakhtin claims results from a deeply involved participation with an alien culture and language.[5] That is, as a French-born, French-speaking child suddenly immersed in an unknown culture, that of Mexico, and later also living in a third linguistic community, an English-speaking school in the United States, Poniatowska has experienced a diversity of cultural climates. In the passage that I quoted in the opening lines of this introduction, the writer testifies to her own awareness of the role that language plays in mitigating differences of class, age, and ethnicity between speakers. In my analysis I address the ways in which her multiple linguistic competencies translate into a critical and dialogic view of the society in which she lives and of her own position in that society.

Bakhtin's discovery of a "plurality of independent and unmerged voices and consciousnesses"[6] in the polyphonic novel as exemplified by Dostoevsky's art leads the Russian theorist to posit a notion of the novelistic hero as self-aware, independent from the author, and not dominated by the author's consciousness. Many writers before and after Bakhtin have attested to a sense that at some point their characters mysteriously begin to develop in directions over which they (the authors) have no control. But intriguing as the idea of autonomous characters is, I have never managed finally to conceive of characters as generating their own creative energy, that is, their own language, outside the languages available to the writer. Further, when Bakhtin characterizes the hero's word as independent and not a mouthpiece of the author's voice, I detect an implication on his part that the author is a stable subject whose own voice is monologic in contrast to the dialogic nature of the written text.

At this point, a different notion of subjectivity may be needed to account better for the crossing of diverse languages and the existence of multiple subjects of enunciation in a given text. Paul Smith's 1988 study of contemporary theories of the subject, entitled *Discerning the Subject*, affords a corrective to Bakhtin's coherent, stable speaking agents. I refer extensively to Smith's work in the analysis of *Hasta no verte Jesús mío* in chapter 2, but I draw him in here briefly to suggest that polyphony in the novel may be the expression not of autonomous characters but rather of the multiple and contradictory subject positions that the writer occupies at a given time. That is, if individual subjectivity is produced by the crossing of many words, if it is, then, itself multivoiced, we may see writing as an inscription of those heterogeneous languages without having to accept a kind of "independence" of the fictional character. It is in this sense that I perceive a unique and semantically rich plurality of voices in the writing of Elena Poniatowska, a plurality which is immensely enhanced by a practice of dialogue sustained over the course of a lifetime. Other issues central to my study, such as her apparent "recuperation" of silenced voices and her "invisibility" in certain texts, also respond in interesting ways to the questions posed by Smith's formulation of subjectivity, as I will show.

Finally, my reading of Elena Poniatowska, and of Mikhail Bakhtin, Paul Smith, and other theorists as well, is grounded in a feminist perspective. Feminist literary and cultural theory is, indeed, the sine qua non of my study. The fundamental restructuring of the ways that we read, write, and live in the world which feminism has motivated in the West in the past three decades underlies every aspect of this project, from my choice of an author to "work on" to my selection of texts and my definition of specific issues to pursue. It is a commonplace to acknowledge the enormous diversity of contemporary feminisms within national boundaries and between cultures, and in my analyses I try to contextualize the references that I make to specific essays and theories. But in a more general sense, I owe an intellectual debt to the revolutionary feminist identification of fundamental problems such as the conflation of the masculine with the human in patriarchal cultures, the constructed nature of gender difference, and the intimate connection between gender, language, meaning, and power in human life. Most important, the feminist inquiry, itself dialogic and open-ended, affirms the potential for change in human relations and rejects a static view of ideology and social structures.

My readings in feminist criticism and theory, primarily literary but also ethnographic and, to a lesser extent, psychoanalytic, find resonances in Elena Poniatowska's writings and in her conversations. Any reader would detect a huge conceptual leap between her early statements about feminine intuition, masculine intelligence, and women as "receptacles" for men and for life[7] and the overtly feminist positions that she has staked out in the past thirty years. Although she shies away from speaking as an "expert" on feminism in Mexico, her woman-centered projects, her contributions to *fem*, and her knowledge of the work of major feminist thinkers define her commitment and her contribution to a consciously feminist critique. Hers is a feminism born in direct confrontation with the social, political, and economic situation of Mexico. It is a practical feminism which responds effectively to concrete situations of repression and explores provisional solutions to intractable problems. And it is, above all, a feminism negotiated in the dialogues which nourish her writing and her social practice.

We can easily identify some of the participants in that dialogue, whether Poniatowska has known them face-to-face or through their written legacy: Simone Weil, Rosario Castellanos, Alaíde Foppa, Josefina Bórquez/Jesusa Palancares, the student activists of 1968, Rosario Ibarra de Piedra, and the women of the Mexico City "September 19th" seamstresses' union, among many others. The traces of their words intersect with the writer's languages at every turn in the textual labyrinth. Like the writing of other feminists working in the so-called Third World, Poniatowska's texts demonstrate an acute awareness of class and ethnicity as factors which determine a multiplicity of feminine oppressions. Her remarkable capacity to hear and to honor other voices does not depend on a facile identity with their stories or their lives. On the contrary, Elena Poniatowska's writing often inscribes the insuperable distance that separates her experience

and aspirations from those of others. Silences and refusals oper-
ate even in long-term relationships such as those between the
author and her friends Josefina Bórquez or Rosario Ibarra de
Piedra. Nevertheless, Poniatowska persists in seeking out alli-
ances based on respect for difference and respect for the validity
of the other's—different—claims for justice.

I have organized my study around four important texts dating
from the interviews of the 1950s to the 1988 novel La "Flor de
Lis."[8] In conjunction with each principal work, I also consider
related or complementary pieces including full-length books,
short stories, and a number of Elena Poniatowska's longer essays. Chapter 1 uses the interviews of Palabras cruzadas to
examine questions of language, authority, and cultural and professional competence in the written records of Poniatowska's dialogues with her prominent male interlocutors. In chapter 2 I focus
on the many competing constructions of "Jesusa Palancares,"
protagonist of Hasta no verte Jesús mío and object of numerous
essays by Elena Poniatowska and by critics of the novel. Paul
Smith's work, to which I have already referred, proves to be useful in understanding Jesusa Palancares as "subject" of/to her
own testimony and the testimony of others. In my analysis of
La noche de Tlatelolco, Elena Poniatowska's best-selling book in
Mexico, I employ theories of intertextuality and the Derridean
notion of framing to interpret the historical survival of "visions
of the vanquished" and the problematic role of the intellectual in
recuperating these "other" histories.

In Elena Poniatowska's short stories and her novel La "Flor
de Lis," the author explores worlds close to home; that is, close
to her own experience as a member of Mexico's economically
privileged class. Chapter 4 studies these semi-autobiographical
texts in order to illuminate what may be at stake in Poniatowska's confrontation with the very real barriers that privilege constructs to self-knowledge and social practice. Both the public
dialogues that form the basis of Palabras cruzadas, Hasta no
verte Jesús mío, and La noche de Tlatelolco and the more intimate conversations recorded in La "Flor de Lis" equally attest to
Elena Poniatowska's extraordinary willingness to cross s/words
with others and with herself.

— THE WRITING OF ELENA PONIATOWSKA —

FACE TO FACE
Interviewing Authority

In 1954, when Elena Poniatowska took her first job with a newspaper and published her first pieces of fiction, she began to live a double life common to the careers of many Spanish American writers, that of journalist and literary author. Whether as a means of financial support, for political reasons, or by vocation, journalism has been a mainstay for notable Spanish American novelists, poets, and dramatists since independence. In Mexico, which produces a number of Latin America's most respected newspapers, the names of José Joaquín Lizardi, Ignacio Manuel Altamirano, Manuel Gutiérrez Nájera, Anita Brenner, Martín Luis Guzmán, Alfonso Reyes, and Elena Poniatowska's contemporaries Luis Spota and María Luisa Mendoza are just a few examples that illustrate this continent-wide phenomenon. Now approaching four decades of experience in journalistic investigation and writing, Poniatowska has a particularly high investment in "el tumulto de ese vivir persiguiendo la noticia,"[1] and her colleagues and readers consider her to be one of the most perceptive chroniclers of contemporary Mexican society.

Therefore, by beginning my study with a discussion of Poniatowska's early years as a journalist, I highlight fundamental aspects of her entire corpus: her production of journalistic, nonfiction texts that stand on their own merit as ground-breaking achievements; the recognition that journalism has nourished in a significant and positive way her writing of novels and short stories; and the importance of the interview, her principal journalistic genre, both in her formation as a writer and as a discourse with its own intrinsic logic and interest. The hundreds of interviews that Poniatowska carried out in the first six years of her career provided a necessary, practical education through which she has learned to recognize (that is, both to perceive and to acknowledge) the many and diverse voices of her country. In this chapter I provide a general characterization of her early interview-articles, and I analyze three of them with a particular focus on the articulation of power and language as reflected in the shifting structures of authority between the two speakers involved.[2]

In the 1950s, as is still true today, the Mexican national press was dominated by publications produced in the capital. *Excélsior* (established in 1917), *El Universal* (1916), and *Novedades* (1935) were the principal daily newspapers, with circulations in 1959 of 120,000, 90,000, and 80,000, respectively. Carlos Monsiváis, in an often scathing critique of the Mexican press, characterizes the news media of the 1940s and 1950s as ideologically homogeneous, proestablishment, nationalistic, virulently anticommunist, moralizing, uncritical, and lacking in analysis of events and even in adequate information about them.[3] A less personally involved foreign commentator writing in the 1950s provides contemporary evidence to support Monsiváis in his portrayal of a press which was largely conservative, generally respectful of the government and public officials, and weak on serious analysis of contemporary issues. Sports, society news, comics, and entertainment figured prominently alongside foreign and national news.[4] Elena Poniatowska confirms these judgments out of her own experience, noting that some public figures paid the political columnists to keep their names out of the gossip mill, while conversely others paid to see themselves mentioned. *Excélsior*, a conservative, Catholic publication which wielded considerable influence on public opinion during the period, embodied a middle-class, pro–United States, pro-Franco, antilabor, and (within decorous limits) antigovernment line. Media criticism of the government was limited in part by the state's ability to control the press through various direct and indirect methods. State regulation of the import and distribution of newsprint, outright subsidies of the newspapers, and the widespread payment of "gratuities" to the low-paid reporters contributed to creating a closed circuit between press and government. Reluctant to bite the hand that feeds, many journalists succumbed to self-censorship.[5]

A 1956 essay on women in Mexican journalism mentions the names of several dozen women journalists working in the period from 1920 to mid-1950. Most were active in the following, familiarly feminine areas: society news, the women's page of newspapers, women's magazines dedicated to domestic life and moral issues, and socially conscious investigative reporting or editorializing on the problems of children, education, and the role of women in society.[6] Female journalists apparently had little involvement in the reporting of politics, finance, military affairs, foreign policy, or crime, suggesting that journalism offered both opportunities and obstacles to women's entry into public discourse. The names of Elena Poniatowska and another writer also known for her interviews, Ana Cecilia Treviño ("Bambi"), appear in the closing paragraph of the essay as examples of promising young women in the national press.[7] University programs in journalism were rare in Latin America until recently, and most male and female reporters of the 1950s and 1960s relied on on-the-job training rather than academic studies for their professional preparation.

This, then, is the general context in which to view Elena Poniatowska's entry into journalism in 1954: an entry that was unremarkable, even stereotypical in many respects, and, at the same time, highly unlikely. Poniatowska got her first jobs (with *Excélsior* in 1954 and *Novedades* one year later) through family acquaintances. A relative of one of her friends was the editor of the society news section of *Excélsior*, and Poniatowska's mother knew Alejandro Quijano, an editor at *Novedades*, through their shared involvement in volunteer activities with the Red Cross. Early opportunities to interview diplomats, intellectuals, and artists also opened up for her through family connections, frequent invitations to society events attended by the elite of Mexico City, and her fluency in the French and English languages, all consequences of her privileged class background. At the same time, Poniatowska began to work, rather than single-mindedly to pursue the social circuit and the road to an early marriage, out of a certain sense of dissatisfaction with the limited standard options available to young women of her social class.

An additional complication for her decision to work in Mexico was the fact that, at age twenty-one, Elena Poniatowska still had very little understanding of Mexican culture and society. Bear in mind her Eurocentric education and the two years of Catholic boarding school in the United States. In fact, her extraordinarily privileged—and equally disadvantaged—situation as she began to work as a journalist in 1954 is just the first of many instances that show privilege to provide both access and obstacle, advantage and limit in Elena Poniatowska's career. The following passage, from an unpublished 1982 interview, highlights several characteristics of Poniatowska's early procedures as an interviewer and evokes a vivid image of her first forays into the world of journalism.

> My decision was a kind of rejection of expectations, because I belong to a well-off, if not reactionary, social class. The goals of women of that class in that time period were to marry, have children, and attend balls.
>
> I spent a year at *Excélsior* and then I changed to *Novedades*. The year of apprenticeship at *Excélsior* helped me a great deal because I did an interview every day. I learned as I went along. I interviewed writers, singers, musicians, everyone. It helped me acquire the knack for dialogue, and it was a way of getting an education that I had not had before. I didn't know who Diego Rivera was, nor Carlos Pellicer, nor Octavio Paz. I didn't know anybody.
>
> I remember that the first questions that I asked stemmed from my complete innocence and ignorance. I asked Diego Rivera, "Why are you so fat? Why do you have such little teeth?" And then out of a naive question came an entire interview and a whole new journalistic style in Mexico. Because in Mexico everyone was very solemn and formal. So for someone to come along and say, "Oh, how fat you are!" was in a certain sense an impertinence but also a new way of doing business.[8]

Seventeen examples of this "impertinent," "new way" of doing things were published in *Palabras cruzadas* (1961), a sampling chosen from the hundreds of her interview-articles which appeared in newspapers between 1954 and 1961.[9] Although Elena Poniatowska reports having had to pay frequent fines for representing public figures irreverently, that is, "without being well-informed about the newspaper's interests,"[10] her readers apparently welcomed the personal tone and the self-deprecating humor with which she portrayed herself in conversation with the "great men" of contemporary culture and politics. Her subjects were primarily Mexican nationals, but she also interviewed many Spanish American and European intellectuals such as Alejo Carpentier, Cesare Zavattini, and François Mauriac.

The importance of the period 1954 to 1961 as a kind of professional apprenticeship and intellectual immersion experience should not be underestimated. From an initial position of ignorance, Poniatowska necessarily and quickly acquired a working knowledge of Mexican culture through her dialogues with many of its most prominent voices. This knowledge, which took Elena Poniatowska far beyond the limits of her Catholic finishing school education, allowed her to begin to live and work responsibly in Mexico. However, her newly expanded perspective on Mexican society and culture was still essentially patriarchal and elitist, even if occasionally critical: a classic "view from above" which the young interviewer was in a weak position to challenge or even, perhaps, to perceive. It is important to keep this in mind in consideration of Poniatowska's reputation as a literary "champion of the oppressed" and, in particular, as an advocate of women's voices and histories. This oft-quoted characterization is based on her better-known projects undertaken a decade and more after the first interviews of *Palabras cruzadas*. Therefore, for many readers the early interviews may appear to be distressingly naive and submissive in tone in contrast to the critical stance which is the hallmark of her later works. Nevertheless, I believe that already in the 1950s Poniatowska demonstrates an aptitude for attentive listening and candid questioning which is one key to her future critique of Mexican institutions and her engagement with the lives and the stories of Mexico's marginalized majority.

The selected texts republished in *Palabras cruzadas*, then, are valuable in a number of ways for the contemporary reader of Elena Poniatowska's writing. They are fascinating documents for the political and cultural history of Mexico, and they anthologize the writing of a one-time "new" voice (now an established authority) in Mexican journalism. The articles could perhaps also be searched for the seeds of Poniatowska's later flowering as an author. My interest in analyzing several of the articles stems from rather different motives, however. As I have described in the introduction, my interpretation of Elena Poniatowska's writing identifies the primacy of dialogue in her texts. Further, in a dialogue, power is often the primary meaning or effect of the verbal exchange. Power to speak, to command attention, and to silence or to encourage speech in the other constitutes the overt or covert agenda of many a conversation, and the dynamics of verbal communication and verbal positioning between the speakers are frequently fraught with issues of control. Remember in this regard that Poniatowska conducted her first interviews with men such as Alfonso Reyes, Lázaro Cárdenas, and Diego Rivera under rather unpromising circumstances: she was a naive, semiforeign, conventionally educated, socially privileged female coming face to face with a series of well-known male public figures, most a generation older than she. At the same time, the status of journalist conferred on Poniatowska a certain measure of authority, and she could legitimately assume a minimum institutional right to ask questions and report the answers.

My analysis explores the power relationships between the two speakers in Elena Poniatowska's idiosyncratic approach to the highly conventionalized journalistic interview. I wish to ask to what extent the hierarchical relationship between the canonized interviewee and the culturally less competent interviewer yields to destabilizing pressures generated through dialogue. I do not believe that Elena Poniatowska started out in this field with the consciously formulated goal of subverting the prestige of her subjects. Indeed, she often writes herself into the articles in the role of an admirer. What does intrigue me about *Palabras cruzadas* is to view the articles as a record of the contestatory potential of dialogue, even when that dialogue is conducted within specific institutional constraints. Is there something inherently "dialogic" in the discourse of conversation? How did Poniatowska's personal history and her approach to the interview event position her in a way that may have either facilitated or blocked acts of resistance on her part to the authority of the speakers she encountered? By pursuing these questions, I hope to provide insights into issues of control and disruption which are central to all of Elena Poniatowska's writing and which are pressing concerns of contemporary feminist theory as well.

In the passage quoted above, Elena Poniatowska sets out some of the terms that defined her position as an interviewer in the 1950s. Youth, ignorance, and naiveté are predetermined constraints on her authority to speak as a professional on an equal footing with her famous subjects. In a 1957 interview conducted by Lya Kostakowsky, the young reporter, here playing the role of reluctant interviewee, testifies to her acute awareness of this asymmetry—and her ability to exploit it. "The fun of my interviews is in part to say nonsense, or to make the poor interviewees say it. Perhaps you can accuse me of overusing the procedure of the idiotic question, but I can respond that asking silly questions is the best way to acquire wisdom." [11] In summary, to initiate and carry on a dialogue, Elena Poniatowska depended on the efficacy of the foolish or trivial question, ingenuousness, spontaneity, wit, and a focus on the personal side of her subjects' lives in order to compensate for a lack of experience or rigorous preparation on her part. Poniatowska does not mention one additional inescapable factor at play here: her femininity. Nevertheless, it is always highly significant that she speaks and is spoken to as a woman among men.

By referring to the pieces collected in *Palabras cruzadas* as "interview-articles" or "interview-based" articles, I have already implied that their textual status is something different from a transcription of a recorded conversation. Whether Poniatowska tape-recorded the interview or took notes by hand, the published article represents a considerable transformation of the initial dialogue. I will take the written article as my object of study without pretending to recuperate the "original" conversation or the unretouched identities of its protagonists. The text is a construct which combines a title, passages of more or less faithfully transcribed speech, clearly differentiated characters, description, and direct address to the reader, all under the control of a narrator who identifies herself with the character of the interviewer. To the extent, however, that the articles do remember and re-present the speech of others, it is fair to say that they include heterogeneous voices which exceed the absolute control and design of the writer. The complex relationship between "truth" and "fiction" in Poniatowska's journalistic, ostensibly factual writing is a constant source of creativity and, perhaps for the reader, confusion. In this chapter I emphasize the constructed nature of the articles over their referentiality in my analysis of issues of language and power.

THE POWER OF SILENCE: FRANÇOIS MAURIAC

Artless ignorance elevated to method may have worked effectively for Elena Poniatowska in disarming many of her interviewees and gaining an entrance to their thoughts. But the pursuit of knowledge through the art of the "idiotic question" can just as easily backfire, ensnaring the interviewer in a dead end of silence whose only exit is reached in retreat. One such experience of failure is recounted, with many an ironic twist, in the aptly titled "Invitación a la puerta" (Shown to the door). Poniatowska published this article in April 1956 after interviewing prolific French novelist, dramatist, and Nobel laureate François Mauriac. She conducted the interview in French at the author's home in Paris, so the resulting article involved an exercise in linguistic and cultural translation as it took shape for a Mexican audience. Like many of her later interviews, the piece incorporates fragments of dialogue, observation, and invention to create a hybrid discourse in which we attend not to the voices of the historical François Mauriac and Elena Poniatowska but to two semifictional characters, Mauriac and an anonymous "señorita."

"Invitación a la puerta" is a concise, carefully constructed article which ostensibly commemorates a fiasco, but it tells the tale in such a way that the text finally stands at cross-purposes with the original conversation, with "experience," with ignorance, and with its own stated preoccupation with silence and failure. Techniques of reversal or inversion give the article its unique structure and condition its ironic effects. Starting with the first question (which was posed, significantly, by the interviewee and not the interviewer), the text continually overturns expectations and defies convention.

> —¿Ha leído usted algunas obras mías?
> —No, señor Mauriac. Apenas voy a comenzar. Ayer compré *Nido de víboras* . . . Pero dígame usted, ¿cuál es su mejor libro?
> —De nada serviría que le conteste, señorita, usted no conoce mi pensamiento. No hay conversación posible . . . (163) [12]

In the opening lines Mauriac refuses dialogue in the absence of the shared knowledge necessary for two speakers to communicate. There simply is no possible (meaningful) conversation to be sought here, and silence descends as "François Mauriac, alto y flaco, se puso a frotarse las manos con impaciencia, bajo el pretexto de que estaba haciendo mucho frío en su biblioteca" (163). [13] This is the moment of speechlessness and powerful, silent gestures, when the young interviewer experiences failure as an indictment of her professional irresponsibility. It is a moment that will have echoes, like the slamming of a door, throughout the text in the numerous variations on one painful theme: "Have you read some of my works?" Beginning at this critical juncture, an apparent dead end, the article advances in fits and starts through reiteration and inversion to allow the interviewer to regain some of her lost authority. The key players are the doubled I of the narrator-protagonist, identified only as "señorita," and François Mauriac. All three figures interact within the written text in a dynamic display of the exercise of authority through language.

The preeminent place given to Mauriac's impromptu question and the reversal of roles which it implies signal its importance in the production of meaning in the text. That the overall composition of the article is not a transcription but an ingenious transformation of the interview between Elena Poniatowska and

François Mauriac becomes clear in the passage immediately following the initial exchange quoted above. To fill the void left by Mauriac's refusal, the narrator inserts an unflattering description of the writer's "figura larga y reseca, el aspecto de fraile decalcificado y amenazante" (long, skinny figure, his threatening appearance of a discalced friar) (163). She then addresses readers directly in an appeal for sympathy and support. Claiming that this is the first time in dozens of interviews that such a thing has happened, she protests that not a single author has ever asked her if she'd read his or her books. Considered in those terms, it is Mauriac who is being unreasonable, and prior experience absolves the interviewer of error, at least, she hopes, in the readers' eyes.

Invigorated by her memories and by a sense of just indignation, the interviewer reappears with a question for Mauriac, but it is another "idiotic question" (about his health) and it meets a similarly dismal fate. In complete silence Mauriac "hizo un leve, casi inconsciente movimiento hacia la puerta, como para invitarme a salir" (made a slight, almost unconscious gesture toward the door, as if inviting me to leave) (163). The first echo of the title sounds in this mute gesture, against which the interviewer's endless chatter has little effect. The conventional associations of voice with power and muteness with subordination are inverted, as Mauriac's most effective means of control is precisely an eloquent, imposing silence. But, excepting an immediate retreat, the only avenue available to the hapless, silenced "señorita" is the insistence of speech, words, questions, which soon take their most servile forms—flattery, pleading, humility—in an attempt to reverse the downward spiral of the tragic ("nefasta") interview. Simultaneously the initial question, innocent enough when first posed, reappears at every opportunity couched in increasingly negative language. Mauriac will not discuss "libros que [usted] no ha leído" (books that you have not read) (164), and the interviewer laments the painful incident over Mauriac's books "que yo no había leído" (166).

Having thus carefully staged the moment of her worst defeat, the narrator turns back in time to recall her arrival at Mauriac's house and the favorable impression caused by the bright sitting room comfortably appointed with white carpet, piano, and paintings. The narrative anachrony highlights her reversal of fortune, a reversal portrayed, ironically, in reverse by telling the story backward from present misfortune to past, squandered fortune. The present impasse not only contradicts the events of a few moments ago at Mauriac's house, but it also projects an inverted image of the interviewer's many previous successes with equally famous writers.

The second half of the brief but tightly written article starts when Mauriac, "a base de ruegos y movido a lástima" (after much pleading and moved to pity) (166), deigns to answer a few questions, without for a moment relinquishing his control of the situation. Speech and silence have different and multiple values for the two participants in the dialogue recreated from the interview. Silence is power for Mauriac, as is speech, because he speaks, or chooses not to speak, from a position of authority based on his superior knowledge and social status. The interviewer is caught between silence and devalued speech (chatter or flattery), both her speech and her silence equally symbolic of her lack of authority and her ignorance. She seems to salvage a minimum right to speak only by playing out her subordinate role to its (typically feminine) limit. The practical potential for disrupting the hierarchical structure of the lopsided exchange looks extremely limited, and dialogue in "Invitación a la puerta" is constantly under threat of foreclosure by Mauriac. Half-articulated thoughts, hesitations, unanswered questions, and Mauriac's tendency to interrogate the interviewer plague the closing scene between them.

Soon all that remains is for the interviewer to formulate a closing question and accept the proffered "invitación a la puerta" with apologies to the severe, unyielding Mauriac. His last words reiterate his dismay, literally dismissing the entire experience as one of boredom and disillusionment for himself and for future readers of the interview. But he does not have the last word, as it turns out. The narrator, writing from beyond the time frame of the interview, testifies to a future, more productive dialogue that she, as a reader now and not as a journalist, has carried on with Mauriac's works. In one last reversal, she asserts

her capacity to overcome ignorance (and silence), a capacity perhaps strengthened on "aquel día de ingrata memoria" (that long-
ago, ill-remembered day) (167). The article itself is a record of
the power of language and silence to dominate when it is exer-
cised by those who enjoy superior status. It also demonstrates
that any encounter with that power which accepts the terms it
imposes, as did the interviewer in this example, will have little
contestatory strength. One must be willing, as Teresa de Lauretis
says, to "'begin an argument' and so formulate questions that
will redefine the context, displace the terms of the metaphors
and make up new ones. That argument is also a confrontation, a
struggle, a political intervention."[14] In 1956 Elena Poniatowska
was ill-prepared for such an intervention, which would depend
on an active engagement with the other and with the world, and
on bringing an accumulated knowledge to bear on experience.
But the overall structure of "Invitación a la puerta" suggests that
Elena Poniatowska's later, more successful confrontations with
authority were made possible by acts of speaking, reading, and
writing in which she acquires knowledge and mediates the discourse of the other for her own ironic, self-critical purposes.

THE MASTER'S VOICE: DIEGO RIVERA

In a succinct formulation of one of the major themes of modern
linguistics, Mikhail Bakhtin wrote that "language is not a neutral medium that passes freely and easily into the private property of the speaker's intentions; it is populated—overpopulated—
with the intentions of others."[15] Elena Poniatowska's interviews
with Mexican muralist Diego Rivera illustrate this social dimension of language in a context which emphasizes the difficulties
that individual speakers may experience precisely when trying
hardest to shape to their own use a language "populated with
the intentions of others." "Añil y carne humana" (1959, Anvil
and human flesh) provides ample evidence that words are, indeed, "born in dialogue" and that they are always at least "half
someone else's," as Bakhtin says. The article reconfirms the lesson of "Invitación a la puerta": that talk is not necessarily dia-

logic, and a face-to-face encounter can easily construct itself as an unequal debate in which the less privileged speaker is severely constrained in his or her access to meaning making and intentionality through language. The other's intentions place strictures on any individual's entry onto the highly contested field of speech.

Elena Poniatowska interviewed Diego Rivera twice in the late fall of 1956. Rivera died the following year, and Poniatowska wrote and published her lengthy article about him in 1959. The time frame is significant, because the relatively long lapse between the interviews and the writing of the piece must have served to distance the writer emotionally from her subject and from the event of their conversations. Published posthumously, moreover, the article functions as a tribute to the ever controversial genius of Mexican painting.

In contrast to "Invitación a la puerta," which begins in media res, the two interviews of "Añil y carne humana" are elaborately framed by an introduction and an extensive concluding section that combines an "Homenaje ante su tumba" and four testimonies about Diego Rivera given by family members and friends. The complex, multifaceted sketch of Rivera—part self-portrait and part representation—creates a verbal mural out of heterogeneous voices. The framing passages and the technique of juxtaposing material from a variety of sources prefigure Poniatowska's procedures in later documentary works, and they respond here to the difficulty of defining Diego Rivera's contradictory personality. As the narrator of "Añil y carne humana" comments, "uno no sabe a qué atenerse con él" (one doesn't know quite what to think of him) (41). The fundamental tension that she targets is that overworked opposition between the public and the private Rivera, or the "myth" and the "man." Poniatowska confronts legend and gossip with her own direct personal observations and with Rivera's speech in an apparent attempt to correct the exaggerated proportions of his larger-than-life image with a more intimate and sympathetic view. However, I believe that the article shows that the split between public perception and private identity is not discernible from any perspective. To pose the dilemma in quintessentially Mexican terms, face and mask do not exist as opposing ontological categories, and the private "I" of Diego Rivera cannot speak free of the constructing gaze of the public "eye."[16]

The article begins at a distance from its subject, with the narrator reiterating and yet poking fun at the popular characterization of Rivera as an artist with superhuman energy and talent, an outspoken supporter of communism, a womanizer, and an imposing physical presence. It took Poniatowska three years to arrange the interviews, and she confesses to feeling intimidated by his reputation. But when she finally meets him, "reality" confounds her expectations, and the man that she thinks she discovers behind the myth both delights and disconcerts her. The first two paragraphs of the piece function as a verbal frame to move us from the outer or the superfluous (legend, gossip) to the heart of the matter (i.e., the interviews themselves). This gesture is embodied, so to speak, in the series of augmentatives with which the narrator describes the body-Rivera: "barrigón," "cabezón," "ojón" (big-bellied, big-headed, bug-eyed). The list ends, appropriately enough, with "corazón," or heart, the metaphorical center of human emotion and Poniatowska's target. It serves her purpose nicely to remember that *corazón* was itself derived etymologically in Spanish as an augmentative of the Latin word *cor*.

After Diego Rivera's death, Elena Poniatowska spoke with a number of his friends and family members in a further, final attempt to go beyond the nonessential Rivera—the womanizer, the communist—and pay homage to the great artist whose most authentic act was to revindicate indigenous Mexico. The testimonies appended to the interview comprise almost half the article's forty pages, without, however, significantly adding to its insights or its interest. Indeed, they are remarkably unsuccessful in revealing either the man or the greatness in the "great man," imbued as they are with resentments and betrayals and largely self-absorbed in tone and content.[17] The lack of integration between the major components of the article (introduction, interviews, testimonies) takes away from the potential effectiveness of framing the reconstructed conversations with perspectives drawn from multiple informants. This leads us back to the two interviews conducted shortly before Diego Rivera's seventieth birthday in December 1956.

While Elena Poniatowska's aim of uncovering the face behind the mask may seem naive, she did have the wisdom to realize that the speaker and his speech are inseparable. In the interview sections of "Añil y carne humana" the narrator states that she tried to preserve Rivera's language, even when muddled, as integral to his thought. By examining his words and the specific context in which he spoke, I believe that we can interpret the important features of his interaction with the interviewer as signs of their asymmetrical access to authority and as signs of the contradictory nature of Diego Rivera as an embodiment of both "progressive" politics and patriarchal values.

The interviews have the tone of a debate, with sharp disagreements arising between the two protagonists, particularly over questions of politics. Throughout the conversation, Diego Rivera has the upper hand, and his meanings and intentions alone determine the choice of topics and the correctness of viewpoint. Male privilege is primordial as a source of Rivera's dominant role in the interviews. He clearly speaks with the master's voice, and he exercises his mastery over words surrounded, literally, by female disciples and subordinates. Besides the interviewer, the other women present at various times during the interviews are Rivera's housekeeper, a giggling young lady who arrives carrying a much pampered lap dog, and several art students—all female and each one "humilde," "mansa," or "suave" (humble, gentle, compliant), according to the narrator. The narrator evokes another important female presence by quoting from the writings of the deceased Frida Kahlo. Frida Kahlo's marriage to Rivera is a major theme of the interview, a theme introduced by Rivera himself. Rivera is thus situated in the text as Man among women, superior among subordinates, and his speech will function as an instrument of mastery.

The interviewer's ability to mount a challenge to that power is doubly limited by the constraints imposed by the situation itself and by her unique status as a speaking subject. Built into the journalistic interview is a predetermined position of authority for the interviewee, as we saw in "Invitación a la puerta." Within that structure Elena, or "Elenita," Poniatowska's youth, femininity, national origin, and social class further position her at the margins of Rivera's discourse; she is the cultural and sexual other to his "I"; the French-Polish *princesa* to his Mexican proletarian-identified muralist. In addition, certain aspects of her own participation affirm Rivera's superiority and thereby signal her complicity in maintaining the status quo. For example, her initial questions in the first interview are general (not specific to Rivera) and focus on personal or private concerns. They could have been asked to anyone, which leaves the door open for Rivera to direct the conversation to topics of his own choosing. Throughout the interviews Elena Poniatowska also addresses the artist as *maestro*, a term of affectionate respect. Thinking back to the description of her early interviews which I have quoted, we see that the trivial questions she recalls having asked Rivera do reappear in this article in the narrator's description of her subject as "barrigón" and in a reference to his "dientes de leche" (baby teeth). She would have us visualize an imposing and yet vulnerable, childlike Rivera, an image, however, which is not well supported by the record of their confrontation.

How does the *maestro* speak? And how does his language serve to define, to control, and to exclude? Three main topics predominate in the two interviews: art, women, and politics. More specifically, Rivera speaks about Mexican muralism, his opinions about women in general and his marriage to Frida Kahlo, and his enthusiasm for Soviet-style communism and the 1956 invasion of Hungary. As recorded by Elena Poniatowska, his discourse favors absolute values, superlative terms, clichés, and idealizing rhetoric to portray reality as a series of opposing—and unequal—categories. The dichotomies male-female and working class—bourgeoisie are the principal categories that structure his discourse and his interaction with the interviewer. Diego Rivera's self-contradictory statements about women are almost too easy a target for a feminist critique, revealing as they do prototypical Latin patriarchal values. Woman is both ideal and servile, man's spiritual superior and his sexual object, central and marginal to human culture. Rivera speaks of his love for

Frida Kahlo as the highest value of his life, he mentions several women scientists and artists among his list of "heroes and heroines," and he even claims that "la humanidad es la mujer. Los hombres somos una subespecie de animales, casi estúpidos, insensitivos, inadecuados completamente para el amor, creados por la mujer para ponerse al servicio [de ellas]" (44).[18] But read in context, his exalted, exaggerated rhetoric is reduced to a trivializing, dismissive gesture toward the "preguntitas" asked by "Elenita." The *maestro* is playing a not very subtle game at his interlocutor's expense, goading her into challenging his outrageous performance while positioning her as unequal to the task. Her follow-up questions and her reactions show how she tries to destabilize his intentions, especially when her personal beliefs and values are threatened, but her contestatory power is limited.

The second interview, which centers on politics and the Soviet invasion of Hungary, offers perhaps the clearest example of the difficulty of subverting the meanings of the master's words from within the master's house. Poniatowska's opening question about Hungary uses a negative formulation in a conventional fashion to elicit an affirmative response. The query "Aren't you shocked at what is happening in Hungary?" positions Rivera to answer "Yes, I am." But contrary to expectations, Rivera declares his enthusiastic support for the events in Hungary, calling them extraordinarily useful and cause for celebration. The theme of cold war Eastern Europe and communism sets interviewer and interviewee on a collision course that lasts for the entire interview. A key tactic of Rivera's verbal assault is his appropriation of the most clichéd vocabulary of Marxist ideology and especially of the (overpopulated) term *pueblo* (people). Speaking of Hungary, Poland, and then of Mexico, Rivera opposes masses (i.e., "obreros," "comunistas," "pueblo" [workers, communists, people]) to masters (i.e., "fuerzas imperialistas," "bandidos imperialistas," "capitalistas" [imperialist forces, bandits, capitalists]) to the greater honor of the former and to his own advantage.

Pueblo means many things for Diego Rivera, and it comes into his domain already semantically loaded, "half someone else's." In the first interview, immediately after identifying himself as one of the *pueblo*, Rivera describes the masses as the "héroe supremo de todo lo que se realiza de positivo en el mundo" (the supreme hero of everything positive that happens in the world) (50). The positive role played by the people in world history, the certainty of their future rise to power via socialist revolution, and their superior courage and moral integrity are the givens of Rivera's social thought, and he places himself squarely within their ranks. Embracing revolutionary elements of the working class, the peasants, and the intellectuals, in a Mexican context *pueblo* also signifies the indigenous people, elevated by Rivera's art to cultural symbols of Mexico's past and future glory. Rivera's many references to the *pueblo* and *lo popular* qualify them as unequivocally good and heroic, often victims but never victimizers, because their violence when it erupts is the necessary, purifying violence of revolution.

A term of such absolute value proves to be a handy weapon in the ensuing debate over contemporary events in Poland and Hungary. By fixing its meaning in accordance with his intentions and casting himself as a key protagonist of the *pueblo*'s historic struggle, Rivera speaks from a position of nearly unassailable authority. Essential categories and articles of faith are notoriously resistant to attack, and Rivera effectively uses *pueblo* as a term of exclusion in his discussion with Elena Poniatowska. For her part, seeing her political opinions and her national loyalties threatened (she, after all, identifies with her own idea of the Polish *pueblo* via her father's ancestry), the interviewer objects vigorously and repeatedly to Rivera's world view. One recourse that she employs is to reiterate a word or a phrase spoken by Rivera in a new context which undermines its earlier meaning.

As the debate unfolds, the master's voice, now impatient, takes on increasingly sarcastic overtones, resorting to personal attack and insulting diminutives to discredit and silence the other. By positioning "Elenita" as non-*pueblo*, traitorous Pole, young, frivolous, and female, he all but denies her any access to knowledge and truth. "Los verdaderos polacos son los que están en Polonia, . . . y constituyen el pueblo, es decir, los obreros y los campesinos, y no los que están aquí en México haciendo entrevistitas" (58–59).[19] The published article records "Elenita's" speechless shock at this particularly cutting rebuke, but it also affords Elena Poniatowska the writer the opportunity for a belated retort. Playfully asserting her own authority, Poniatowska has subtitled the second interview "Diego Rivera no tiene remedio" (Diego Rivera is a hopeless case).

It is evident that Poniatowska brings both more information and more strongly held opinions to her encounters with Diego Rivera than she did to her interview with François Mauriac. She will not be silenced, nor does the other refuse to engage her in a dialogue, although he is able to conduct it more or less on his own terms. Perceived by Rivera as his social and political adversary, the interviewer-narrator tries to intervene positively on her own behalf. But most of her measures are defensive and fail to open up the debate to any significant degree. Monologic discourse which posits absolute values, fixed meanings, and mutually exclusive semantic categories seems to be effective in upholding established structures of authority, at least at the moment of speaking. Perhaps only from a distance can the Diego Rivera of "Añil y carne humana" be seen as a contradictory figure whose progressive political ideas and hopes for the *pueblo*'s future liberation are framed by an oppressive, patriarchal discourse and *machista* posturing. As readers we may be in an advantageous position to make those judgments based on our own ideological formation, but we must pay tribute to the journalist's role in eliciting and mediating a richly suggestive record of the other's language.

FAINT PRAISE: ALFONSO REYES

In May 1959, three years after interviewing François Mauriac and Diego Rivera, Elena Poniatowska interviewed another towering figure of Mexican intellectual life, Alfonso Reyes. In the article "Don Alfonso en su palomar" (Don Alfonso in his dovecot), the journalist demonstrates a noticeably more professional attitude toward her task. She has read some of Reyes' works, she has prepared a series of pertinent questions, and it is clear that she is familiar with the author's place in Mexican letters and his role in national affairs. Alfonso Reyes, for his part, proves to be a willing, even enthusiastic, participant in the interview, ready to answer any question and good-naturedly volunteering humorous anecdotes about his life and career. Nothing of the gloom of "Invitación a la puerta" or the stridency of "Añil y carne humana" threatens the pleasant atmosphere in Alfonso Reyes' library. However, in no other of Poniatowska's interviews that I have read is the interviewer herself so completely diminished or erased as a presence in the text as she is on the light-hearted pages of "Don Alfonso en su palomar." I would like to suggest that the conditions and the manifestations of her self-effacement reveal much about the subject positions occupied by Elena Poniatowska at that time, and, specifically, how her acceptance of male privilege and her own class privilege makes her conform to the image of conventional femininity projected onto her by her male interlocutor.

Contemporary theories of subjectivity reject notions of a permanent, essential identity or a conscious, coherent, knowing "I" and seek to explain human agency in terms of the many competing and provisional subject positions which a person occupies at a given moment.[20] If we take the interview to be, like any conversation, a social event, we may consider how each speaker is constituted within the event according to his or her personal history and the conditions of the present exchange. Within any dialogue each participant is both a speaking "I" and a spoken "you." That is, each speaker positions him/herself and simultaneously positions the other and responds to an image of him/herself projected by the other. Each is determining and determined, "subject" in the sense of agent and (subjected) object of speech and gesture. In a written article such as Elena Poniatowska's interviews, most of the nonverbal dimensions of that process are lost, and the dialogue has been "subjected" to an unknown amount of editing. The text nevertheless offers a version of the writer-narrator's self-image under pressure from her interlocutor. Such pressure is always reciprocal to some degree, but in the interviews that we have been studying the interviewer seems to exert considerably less influence than she absorbs, for reasons I have already begun to outline. In "Don Alfonso en su palomar" this phenomenon is particularly striking, as Reyes' expectations for

Elena Poniatowska weigh heavily on her participation, and they have that force precisely because they coincide so closely with the class and gender ideology of her personal history.

As in "Añil y carne humana," "Don Alfonso en su palomar" opens at a distance from its famous subject. Again, Poniatowska has been prepared for her meeting with Alfonso Reyes by what other people have told her about him. That her informants are female members of her own family (mother and aunt) lends their testimony special credence and casts the scene in a familiar configuration: the great man surrounded by adoring, infantilized women. In the introductory paragraphs we also meet the two or three *poetisas* who consult with Reyes over any frivolous, pseudo-literary question they can dream up just to enjoy his gallantries. Alfonso Reyes' wife, Manuelita, makes an appearance, seconding her husband's opinions and winking at hints of his past infidelities. It is no wonder that Alfonso Reyes, "que a veces se muestra reservado ante los hombres, o algo severo en sus juicios . . . frente a la mujer no tiene más que ternura" (11),[21] when women are so sweetly and docilely at his service. The problem of women's complicity in their own subordination is acutely, though not, I believe, consciously, portrayed by the writer in this article, which shows all its female characters in positions of happy dependence. The rewards for remaining thus placed are benevolence, gentlemanly courtesies, and support (financial, emotional) from the charming and powerful "don Alfonso."

There is little in the text to suggest that the interviewer, or later the narrator, either perceived or constructed the above-described scene with anything in mind other than the stated intention to praise Alfonso Reyes on the occasion of his seventieth birthday. The entire article is structured to highlight Reyes' prestige as a writer and a cultural leader in Mexico. The opening section positions the interviewer and her informants at a distance from and beneath the central figure; socially, intellectually, and physically subordinate to him. His first words quoted from the interview are, significantly, "¡Me perdonas que no baje, pero aquí estoy, como un loro subido en su estaca!" (Forgive me for not coming down, but here I am like a parrot up on his perch!) (12). Atop a library ladder and surrounded by the books and papers of his enormous collection, the interviewee towers over the scene, while the interviewer and the readers remain below, eyes and voices uplifted in an attitude of veneration. To explain in more detail the pressures that construct a position of submission and silence for the I-narrator-interviewer, I will use this article and other sources to illustrate the two principal forces operating on the subject(ed) "I" of Elena Poniatowska. These forces are the image that Alfonso Reyes projects onto her (the "you" to whom he imagines he speaks) and the interviewer's class and gender-determined self-image.

The speakers' respective physical positions during the interview establish a hierarchical relationship between them which is immediately reinforced by their asymmetrical usage of the familiar *tú* and the more formal *usted* to address one another. Reyes further positions himself as father and teacher by calling his interlocutor *chiquita* or *hijita*, both child and property (daughter) of the patriarch. He regales her with amusing anecdotes framed in terms familiar to parent-child interaction and she responds, completely in character, applauding him and always asking for just one more story. The constant telling of anecdotes itself encourages passivity in the listener, contributing to making this article the most unilateral or monologic of the interviews. It is one of many ways in which masculine activity and feminine passivity are inscribed in the text and left unchallenged. When speaking of weightier matters (literature, primarily) Reyes wonders aloud if his interlocutor might not be getting bored. The narrator additionally notes that her subject speaks slowly, as if to a small child or to anyone not linguistically competent (a student? a foreigner? Elena Poniatowska could be construed as both).

Other asymmetries are equally striking and equally significant for positioning the interviewer as child/subordinate. Reyes never addresses her by name, whereas the interviewer invokes "don Alfonso" an astonishing forty-two times in fifteen pages of text. The use of the first-person pronoun and first-person verb forms by both speakers is also consistent with the structure of authority already discerned. In contrast to Reyes' emphatic overuse of the pronoun *yo* (judged by standard Spanish usage) and his identification with a wide variety of activities, the interviewer is rarely the subject of any verb, and those few generally designate acts of silent, private meditation or perception.

Structurally and linguistically, the text of "Don Alfonso en su palomar" is unyielding in its representation of the unequal relationship between its two main characters. Alfonso Reyes exercises his authority to speak and to determine to whom he speaks from a position of virtually monolithic prestige, and he seems to rob Elena Poniatowska of even the limited agency that she demonstrates on other occasions. Both this interview and other statements made by Elena Poniatowska identify some of the conditions that may have made the reporter a willing accomplice to Alfonso Reyes' discourse. Again, it is not necessary to read the article as a neutral transcription of a "real" event or a "true" portrayal of the historical Alfonso Reyes to interpret it as a version of real, linguistically coded relationships. That is, whether or not Reyes said all that the text records in just the recorded form is less important than to consider that Elena Poniatowska wrote or mediated the experience according to certain subject positions which are discernible insofar as they are, in turn, inscribed in the published piece or in other available texts.

In reading this article along with many other texts by Elena Poniatowska, several terms stand out as signs of the ambivalent conjunction of gender subordination and race and class privilege in her personal history. For example, when explaining the impracticality and the expense of moving Reyes' collection of books to Cuernavaca, the narrator comments, "Y ni modo que los fueran cargando él y Manuelita, como esos inditos que uno ve pasar por la carretera acarreando pesadísimas ollas de aguamiel" (21–22).[22] Opposed to the unimaginable scene of the creole intellectual and his wife hauling their own books, we are supposed to accept the absolute naturalness of the everyday sight of *inditos* transporting goods to market, dependent on manual labor for survival. The writer-narrator assumes for herself, for Reyes, for the women around him, and for the reader the class privilege, linked to race privilege, that protects "us" from similarly dehumanizing work. I do not believe that the text asked its bourgeois Mexican readers of the late 1950s to question that distinction; on the contrary, it allowed them to feel a sense of security about its rightness.

A second example comes from a story that Elena Poniatowska has told on herself and which invariably comes to my mind as I think about the articles of *Palabras cruzadas*. She has spoken of how, as a young woman, or more properly a young *lady*, she always wore white gloves everywhere. "I used to go to the jail-house wearing white gloves! It didn't matter what might happen to me as long as I had those white gloves on. That's etiquette for you." [23] White gloves: a bourgeois convention of dress, apparel worn by those who don't have to get their hands dirty; femininity as leisure, purity, Hispanic *limpieza*, honor, vulnerability (so hard to keep clean!). The wearing of white gloves, literally or metaphorically, defines a lady and constrains the wearer to polite acts and decorous, decorative speech. Going back to "Don Alfonso en su palomar," the amiable tone masks an a priori acceptance of patriarchal structures by both participants. Elena Poniatowska keeps the gloves on, and Reyes, perched safely atop the seemingly stable apparatus of power, bestows a paternalistic benevolence which treacherously sweetens the subordinate role of the other. Finally, as an homage the Reyes interview offers only faint praise to its subject: faint because it is voiced as an echo of Reyes' own authority and pride against the smooth surface of the interviewer's acquiescent silence.

BEYOND EXPECTATIONS: REMARKS

The articulation of power and language is an ancient theme in all of the discourses of human knowledge and belief. Looking back half a millennium in the Hispanic tradition, we find that Spanish linguist Antonio de Nebrija understood well the power of language and the language of power. In the prologue to his 1492 grammar of the Castilian language, he addressed Queen Isabel, sponsor of Columbus' historic voyage to the west, with these linguistically and politically astute words: "Cuando bien conmigo pienso, mui esclarecida Reina . . . una cosa hállo y sáco por conclusión mui cierta: que siempre la lengua fue compañera del imperio, y de tal manera lo siguió, que junta mente comencaron, crecieron y florecieron y después junta fue la caída de entrambos."[24] In identifying the interdependent fortunes of empire and idiom, Nebrija emphasized language's utility as an instrument of conquest and imperial consolidation, but he recognized as well the vulnerability of both language and empire to change; that is, their vulnerability to reversal of fortune and loss of power.

Almost five hundred years later, French-born future Mexican writer Elena Poniatowska would learn Spanish, the native tongue of Mexico, from subaltern, (doubly) "native" speakers: peasant women of indigenous ancestry. Elena Poniatowska was empowered by their lessons to begin to imagine and realize her own social and cultural identity as a Mexican, in contrast to her family's Francocentric orientation. For her parents, Spanish, once the language of the colonizer, has become the language of the colonized and the subordinate, which their daughter learns, and learns to love, contrary to their expectations: "Here I learned Spanish quickly from the servants, which explains my attachment to the maids, or whatever you want to call them. It explains my fondness for Jesusa Palancares. I learned Spanish because I didn't have to learn it. It was the language of the colonized, not a language that one needed to speak."[25] But linguistic competence, as we have seen, is defined by far more than the acquisition of a language; and Poniatowska, for reasons of class, culture, and gender position, was as often overpowered as empowered by words in the public arena of the interview in the 1950s. Curiously, when I first read the articles of *Palabras cruzadas*, I didn't expect to reach precisely that conclusion. Knowing of her reputation for bringing a new, "impertinent" approach to the interview genre and already familiar with writings such as *La noche de Tlatelolco* and *Fuerte es el silencio*, I hypothesized that the early interviews would more strongly predict the challenge that the later texts pose to hegemonic discourse.[26] In a certain sense, then, my reading falls far short of expectations, but I would like to reevaluate my initial assumptions by posing a final question of my own: How propitious a site was the journalistic interview for countering the voices of the masters which it is intended to serve and for opening a discursive space where new voices might test their authority?

The interviews contained in *Palabras cruzadas*, and they represent only a tiny fraction of the hundreds that Poniatowska carried out, show a degree of informality that stood at odds with the style of writing then prevalent in newspapers such as *Excélsior* and *Novedades*. But many inhibiting factors combined to discourage the subversive potential of that stance on the part of the interviewer. Elena Poniatowska's relative lack of preparation and knowledge gave her a fresh perspective on people and events, but it also proved to be an obstacle to rigorous analysis of them. Her social class affiliation and her finishing school education created a regard for authority and forms which was deeply ingrained in the "white gloves" mentality. A certain complicity is inevitable in carving out a niche as a chronicler of high society events and an interviewer of famous personalities. Thirty years later, Elena Poniatowska commented that her cordial relationship with intellectuals was at one time based on playing their game. "I never felt any resistance as long as I did what the intellectuals thought I should do, namely, advertise for them. I interviewed them for a very long time, and that always pleased them. I was docile, and I continue being docile."[27]

In light of her later books, we tend to read irony into Elena Poniatowska's claim of meek docility, but the lesson of her early interviews predicts Audre Lorde's eloquent and cautionary charge that "the master's tools will never dismantle the master's house. They may allow us temporarily to beat him at his own game, but they will never enable us to bring about genuine change. And this fact is only threatening to those women who still define the master's house as their only source of support."[28] Conversely, genuine change will not be achieved either without understanding the master's tools—and in particular the master's voice. *Palabras cruzadas* is a record not only of patriarchy's power but of one woman's wider experience in the social milieu which was a necessary condition for her later questioning of that power. The fact alone of working and thus breaking with familial expectations, although it was not by any means a violent break, was a significant step for Elena Poniatowska. When she first started at *Excélsior* and *Novedades* she was dismissed by her colleagues as a young woman dabbling at writing and not to be taken seriously. Through perseverance and commitment she gradually earned their acceptance and respect, although within the limits assumed to be proper for a female journalist. In the interviews themselves, lopsided though the dialogues often were, Poniatowska gained a whole world of ideas that challenged her ideological formation. Diego Rivera, for example, in spite of his dogmatism offered a critical view of the United States and capitalism and an analysis of art and politics which took into account social class and economic conditions: ways of thinking which were diametrically opposed to Poniatowska's conservative Catholic individualism. In the Reyes interview we may detect the spark of many ideas which Elena Poniatowska has made uniquely her own over the years: literature as a dialogue with the reader and the vision of Mexico "no [como] un ente abstracto sino un 'hacer' y un 'hacerse'" [(not as an abstract entity, but a "making" and a "becoming") (25). Hundreds of other interviews provide their own lessons, the most important being the very capacity for work and for dialogue that characterizes Poniatowska's career. That capacity will be tested a short decade later, as the Mexican student movement of 1968 and Elena Poniatowska's *La noche de Tlatelolco* provide a tragic testimony to the power of dialogue to disturb the status quo and the power of monologue to defend it, beyond anyone's expectations.

∾

CREATIVE CONFUSIONS
Readings of 'Hasta no verte Jesús mío'

∾

H*asta no verte Jesús mío,*[1] Elena Poniatowska's "first novel," has sparked an explosion of critical commentary and controversy thus far unmatched by the attention paid to any other of the author's works.[2] Its publication in 1969 and the awarding of the Premio Mazatlán de Literatura in 1970 set off a chain reaction of inquiries and analyses which seems to grow under the power of its own self-renewing energy. *La noche de Tlatelolco* may be Elena Poniatowska's best-selling book in the Mexican market, but *Hasta no verte Jesús mío* has generated the most intense interest among "professional" readers.[3] Why? Because it is surrounded by a forcefield of confusion. Confusion over how it was written; confusion over the distinction between Jesusa Palancares (character) and Josefina Bórquez ("real life" referent); confusion over the book's genre (novel? testimony? testimonial novel?); confusion over its ideological value and its aesthetic effects: this is rich fare for the academic consumer.

The result is that today I, or any interested reader, must approach *Hasta no verte Jesús mío* through an entanglement of competing and complementary discourses. The early reviews of the novel, Elena Poniatowska's frequent references to it in speeches, interviews, and essays, and many critical articles and conference presentations altogether constitute inexhaustible readings of *Hasta no verte Jesús mío*. These readings are inexhaustible precisely because they are founded on a productive confusion: a confusion which has its origin in a spilling and mixing (*fundere*) of languages and stories, and a further confusion of writing practices (fact, fiction, interview, invention). *Hasta no verte Jesús mío* remains an open book after almost twenty-five years and a book to which its writer and its readers return time and again, because it destabilizes individual identities (Jesusa Palancares, Josefina Bórquez, Elena Poniatowska) and crosses conventional literary boundaries. The writings which now accompany *Hasta no verte Jesús mío* in my reading and rereading offer insights that enhance our enjoyment and understanding of the text, without diminishing its amply demonstrated capacity for continuing to provoke controversy. In that spirit my study, far from clearing away confusions as if they were cognitive cobwebs to be swept aside, attends to confusion as a productive energy and a snare for the imagination. I regard the novel, its central character, Elena Poniatowska's discourse "about" them both, the irrecuperable but nonetheless real speech of Josefina Bórquez, and the existing criticism all as crisscrossing threads which weave a marvelous net, both instrument of entrapment and elusive object of our contemplation.

A PENULTIMATE VERSION OF JESUSA PALANCARES

When I think about Jesusa Palancares, the narrator-protagonist of *Hasta no verte Jesús mío*, in connection with the many, often conflicting interpretations of her character that I have read, an essay by Jorge Luis Borges comes to mind. In "La penúltima versión de la realidad" (1928, The penultimate version of reality) Borges pokes playful fun at the human need to order the universe by revealing the inadequacy of all our systems of classification, whether complex or simple. In the face of "incalculable and enigmatic reality" (40, my translation), our limited individual powers of comprehension will always fall short of taking full measure of a collectively constructed world. I share Borges' suspicion of fixed categories and precise calculations at the same

time as I recognize, in another Borges creation, his poor, para-
lyzed "Funes el Memorioso," the practical necessity of those
same limits, classifications, even forgetfulness for the processes
of human thought. It is perhaps strange to evoke the sophisticated, metaliterary writing of Jorge Luis Borges in conjunction
with Elena Poniatowska's portrait of an illiterate *mestiza* Mexican woman. But at the very least I owe a debt to the Argentini-
an's title, which I have appropriated to underscore the provisional nature of any version of the "real" and even any version
of a single creative act and its repercussions. Beginning with my
first reading of *Hasta no verte Jesús mío* I have found Jesusa
Palancares to be a provoking, haunting character in all her many
reincarnations. Haunting is the language of her solitude, her
strength, and her resentment. Haunting, too, are the tensions
between her rebelliousness and her conformity, her severity and
her generosity, because they express a terrible ambivalence toward life and toward her condition as a poor woman of mixed
race in contemporary Mexico. Among the diverse accounts of
that life, the novel itself constructs the most complex and compelling image of Jesusa, and with uncounted readings behind me
I find myself still engaged in a dialogue with *Hasta no verte Jesús
mío* and composing yet another, penultimate version of Jesusa
Palancares. In this chapter I will move from a text-centered to a
contextual study of the book in order to push that dialogue in
new directions.[4]

Many readers have accompanied Jesusa Palancares in her
sixty-odd-year journey through contemporary Mexican history.
It is a journey traveled along the margins of Mexican society and
narrated from a position constrained by multiple oppressions.
Born at the turn of the century, poverty and the early death of
her mother mark Jesusa's girlhood, while the violence of the
Mexican Revolution of 1910 decisively shapes her adolescent
years and her bitter, short-lived marriage. The adult Jesusa Palancares, widowed, illiterate, and "unskilled," yet far from ignorant in any sense of the word, settles in Mexico City, where
she supports herself with a variety of low-paying jobs as a live-
in servant, waitress, factory worker, health-care aide, beauty
shop operator, and laundry woman. She experiences varying

kinds and degrees of exploitation in all her employment, and she maintains her economic independence only at great physical and psychological cost. Her conversion to the Obra Espiritual, a popular spiritualist sect, provides Jesusa with a source of empowerment and an alternative religious community to the Catholic Church, which she severely criticizes for abusing its spiritual authority and exploiting the poor.

The indomitable if cantankerous spirit and the surprising behavior of this unconventional protagonist have provoked a wide range of critical and analytical responses. Early studies of the novel discovered in Jesusa Palancares both a model feminist heroine and a failed revolutionary,[5] establishing two ideological poles between which later analyses would locate themselves.[6] Jesusa Palancares has also been studied according to Jungian archetypes and the standards of the picaresque, the neopicaresque, the Hispanic tradition of the *esperpento*, the *Bildungsroman*, and medical anthropology; and each theoretical approach provides fresh insights into the constitution of the literary character and the construction of the literary-critical reading.[7] But virtually all the existing work has one thing in common: it regards Jesusa Palancares as a single, unified narrative and ideological element of the text, an internally consistent subject who sees, acts, and speaks throughout the novel with a single eye, a single mind, and a single voice. Numerous articles trace the development or "evolution" of her character, of course, but the analyses regularly assume that the narrator-protagonist of *Hasta no verte Jesús mío* is one figure in possession of a coherent, conscious subjectivity. My own version of Jesusa Palancares starts with the premise that she is at least a doubled if not a tripled figure, a textually and ideologically split self; a seeing I, and an acting I, and a speaking I who exist not as coordinates of a stable identity but as forces engaged in a relationship marked by tension, contradiction, and separation. Jesusa Palancares is, by this view, not one but many subjects in constant conflict with society and with her own past and present selves.

Gérard Genette defines the fundamental disjunction between fictional I-narrators and protagonists in his description of the autodiegetic text.[8] According to Genette, the narrator of what is traditionally called a first-person novel both is and is not the same as the protagonist of the action, because the I that they share is double.[9] Although linked by a single pronoun and name and sharing biographical data, the narrator and the protagonist are distinct narrative entities, delineated by a series of differences and distances. The very process of self-narration and self-creation is fundamentally determined by separation more than by identity. In addition, the novel *Hasta no verte Jesús mío* is told in retrospect, a situation which increases the distance between narrator and protagonist. As a lucid speaker who remembers and examines her own past life from the perspective of her present knowledge, Jesusa Palancares "sees" the errors, the ignorance, and the accomplishments of her younger self through the distorting lens of memory.[10] Further, the temporal distance between narrator and protagonist is not fixed but fluctuates during the course of the novel according to the changing age of the heroine. The narrator and the protagonist are, then, the same and other, their one life story becoming two or more as the narrating activity assumes a life of its own and the apparent unity of speaker and actor splits apart. In *Hasta no verte Jesús mío*, the relationship between the present speaking I and her past spoken selves is characterized by particular anxieties and antagonisms which, I believe, are significant elements in the novel's version of Jesusa Palancares and her struggle for survival and independence in patriarchal society.

A second set of premises also infuses my reading of *Hasta no verte Jesús mío* as a representation of a life subjected to multiple oppressions. The questions of narrative perspective and the construction of Jesusa Palancares as a subject of action and language in the text are complicated by a consideration of the notion of the subject itself. Paul Smith's excellent recent study of contemporary theories of subjectivity addresses the complexity of our common usage of the term *subject*, which encompasses the opposing meanings of controlling consciousness and object of study, originary agent and determined product of ideology. In the preface to *Discerning the Subject* (1988), Smith uses the contradictions inherent in the phrase "individual subject" to illustrate the irreconcilably split nature of the human subject, which is both discerning agent and "cerned" object of social formations.[11] Far from attempting to heal that split or to hypothesize a future human wholeness, Smith emphasizes the idea (not original to him) that each person occupies many subject positions at a given time and place. These subject positions, which are determined by the prevailing and competing ideologies of a society, are always provisional, partial, and mutually contradictory. Smith suggests that the inevitable contradictions which we must embrace as we inhabit conflicting roles in our lives may account for the potential for social change through individual and collective intervention into hegemonic structures. That is, from within a uniquely constituted personal history, the human agent confronts ideological pressures and intervenes in the status quo. The possibility of socially purposive intervention in the world by individuals is crucial to any theory that wishes to account for social change and for the role of the oppressed as agents of change. However, whether one's intervention takes the form of resistance or conformity or both is an open question which gives telling answers when put to a concrete case. The narrator-protagonist of *Hasta no verte Jesús mío*—female, poor, peasant, then working-class, *mestiza*, illiterate, elderly subject of discourse—responds with ambivalent defiance to this or any interrogation that our reading might pose. Resistance and conformity to the status quo are in constant tension throughout the novel and are nowhere more apparent than in the dynamics of narrative voice and the divided nature of the narrated and narrating I's of Jesusa Palancares.

> Esta es la tercera vez que regreso a la tierra, pero nunca había sufrido tanto como en esta reencarnación ya que en la anterior fui reina. Lo sé porque en una videncia que tuve me vi la cola. Estaba yo en un Salón de Belleza y había unas lunas de espejo grandotas, largas, desde el suelo hasta arriba y en una de esas lunas me vi el vestido y la cola.[12]

With this startling revelation of past lives, present reincarnation, and powers of clairvoyance, the narrator of *Hasta no verte Jesús mío* begins to tell the story of her (third) life. Jesusa's need to explain her present suffering as a fall from past glory immediately takes her well beyond first-person narration's conventional limits—the infancy and the imminent death of the protagonist. In addition, Jesusa the narrator restages the familiar story of paradise lost (but not forgotten) in the popular spaces of the beauty shop and the comic theater: Pierrot and Columbine reflected in salon mirrors. The opening paragraph of the novel thus introduces the reader into the magical and yet harshly earthbound world of Jesusa Palancares, and it illustrates the functional split between the narrating I and the narrated I through the simple use of verb tenses. The I of "regreso" and "lo sé" is the same and other with respect to the I of "fui reina," while the subject of "me vi la cola" mediates the temporal distance between them. Throughout the novel the speaking, seeing, and acting I's of Jesusa Palancares interact in a complex play of difference and identity. At times, the recreated scenes and dialogues almost erase these differences as present and past seem to fuse into a single living memory, but more commonly the narrator and her past selves are sharply distinguished or even at odds with each other.

The divided nature of Jesusa Palancares shows up clearly in the association of the narrator and the protagonist with two separate, well-defined temporal and spatial spheres. The aging narrator speaks from a here and now which does not change in the course of the novel. Spatially confined to her tiny room lost in the slums surrounding Mexico City, the narrating I is also temporally trapped in a strangely instantaneous present moment. Genette observes that in autodiegetic texts, the narrator's storytelling, no matter how drawn out, is a temporal situation with an atemporal essence, an action which may be dated but is not measured and so may pass unnoticed.[13] In *Hasta no verte Jesús mío* the persistent reiteration of the adverbs "here" and "now" reminds the reader of the narrator's perspective on past events, while denying the duration of her speaking activity.

In contrast to the narrator, the I of the protagonist exists in time, and her experiences trace a vast personal and social trajectory: infancy, adolescence, and maturity are projected against the background of six decades of Mexican history. The space that the protagonist occupies is equally large and varied, as her constant migrations, first with the revolutionary army and later in search of employment and a place to live, offer a panoramic vision of Mexico. But the reading of the novel yields a curious result in light of the spheres assigned to the narrator and the protagonist. From within her limited space and apparently without temporal existence, the narrator, and not the protagonist, occupies the primary narrative plane. The speaking I of the narrator intrudes on every page of the novel, interrupting the scenes to comment, judge, anticipate future events, and address her public, as the following passage shows. The context for the fragment is Jesusa's childhood and a description of her father's attempts to keep her older brother, Efrén, out of trouble.

"Mi papá quiso evitarle las malas compañías *como yo a Perico*, pero con todo y eso, él siempre las agarró. Así es que ya el que nace de mala cabeza, ni quien se lo quite" (27, my emphasis).[14] The abrupt mention of Perico is an instance of foreshadowing, a common anachronism in autodiegetic texts.[15] The name Perico appears completely out of temporal sequence but in close association with the trials of raising young boys, and it anticipates Jesusa's adoption of an orphan (Perico) many years after the childhood episode of Efrén's misbehavior. It is therefore the narrator, and not the young protagonist, who draws the connection between her brother and her adopted son, a blurring of identities across time which is reinforced by the referential ambiguity of the phrase "él siempre las agarró." The mixing of two times and two characters in one brief recollection underscores the current preoccupations of Jesusa (her concern for Perico), and it shows how different times are integrated or confused in the narrator's mind. The same passage also contains an example of her tendency to insert her judgments openly into the narrative, often in the form of popular wise sayings.

The narrator's intrusive presence is one of the outstanding features of the book's structure. Jesusa's constant imposition of herself between reader and story could be interpreted as a disruptive force, an obstacle to the illusion of immediacy in the recreation of scenes and the development of other characters. But the explicit intervention of the narrator can be justified by the logic of the whole text. In *Hasta no verte Jesús mío*, the act of narrating, understood as self-creation and even self-salvation, is primordial. The protagonist, for all her adventures and her struggle, would remain just one forgotten face in a crowd were it not that as a speaking subject she reclaims her past and ensures her survival. The speaking I is rightly, then, the more memorable and vital figure as she scolds, fusses, and shouts her way across the pages of *Hasta no verte Jesús mío* and into history.

The shifting relationship between narrator and protagonist to which I have alluded is, in part, simply a consequence of the variable time interval that separates the single present moment of narrating from the many different past moments of the story. Through the power of memory and speech the narrator is "free to slide up and down the time axis that connects [her] two selves." [16] In *Hasta no verte Jesús mío*, however, this relationship is not merely unstable or changing but is peculiarly and significantly charged with conflict and tension. The narrator expresses a striking ambivalence or unease toward her past actions and toward her own survival which I read as a function of the novel's portrayal of Jesusa Palancares as both a dominated subject and a contestatory agent in Mexican society. The predominant ideologies of patriarchal, capitalistic, Catholic, Hispanic Mexico interpolate Jesusa—woman, impoverished, *mestiza*—into multiple and simultaneous oppressed positions. The narrator-protagonist is only partially aware of social class, gender, ethnicity, and, finally, age as interconnected factors in her oppression, although she protests loudly against the real limits that she daily confronts. Jesusa has had to take responsibility for her own survival since childhood, and it is as a practical consequence of the day-to-day struggle that she intervenes in society. Therefore Jesusa's "purposive intervention," to use Paul Smith's term, takes the form of rebellion and resistance, as well as conformity and even defense of traditional values. Some of the conflicting interpretations of the novel and its narrator-protagonist that I have cited may themselves be attempts to reconcile these competing tendencies. In my view, *Hasta no verte Jesús mío* does not encourage such a reconciliation; rather, it invites us to confront the very contradictions that Jesusa Palancares inhabits and to see them as a source of her agency.

The novel is divided into twenty-nine sections which, after the first one dealing with the theme of reincarnation, recount the protagonist's life story in roughly chronological order. The narrator's frequent intrusions interrupt the flow of events without significantly disturbing the progression from childhood to maturity. Although the narrator never gives her year of birth (formal records are often lacking for poor children) and she accounts only vaguely for the passage of time, her allusions to historical events allow us to date her birth at about 1900. The narrator has some persistent memories of her mother, who died when the protagonist was five or six years old, but Jesusa's childhood is dominated by her father's influence and by the constant moves and changes in the family group dictated by the poverty in which they live. Opportunities for formal schooling are conspicuously absent, and the child's practical training in hygiene and household chores is rather haphazardly handled by her father, an older sister, and a succession of "stepmothers." Felipe Palancares' assumption of care for his children after his wife's death partially mitigates their sense of abandonment, and it contrasts strikingly with the narrator's depiction of the Mexican male as generally neglectful of his offspring. However, the overall record of Felipe Palancares' relationship with his children is highly ambiguous, showing evidence of abuse as well as protection.[17]

Jesusa is an aggressive, boisterous child who imitates her father and acts as much as possible like "one of the boys." She gets her first job at the age of ten or eleven when her stepmother, Evarista Valencia, literally gives her to the family of a well-off pharmacist. The girl works as a maid and later cares for their small grandchildren in exchange for room and board. After several years she is reunited with her father, now a soldier with the Carrancista army, and she spends her adolescence accompanying the troops in their constant migrations throughout Mexico. When she is fifteen, her commanding officer forces her to marry an army captain, Pedro Aguilar. Her marriage to the violent Aguilar, with the subsequent loss of liberty and frequent physical and emotional abuse, is the most bitter period of her life. It ends when Pedro is killed in battle, and Jesusa, a widow at age seventeen, never remarries. During most of the next forty years Jesusa

Palancares lives in Mexico City, experiencing periods of relative comfort as well as periods of extreme need and suffering. Combative and at times a heavy drinker, she lands in jail more than once, although her conversion to the Obra Espiritual encourages sobriety and a faith in curative spiritual powers.

Friendships, family ties, possessions, residences, jobs, and adoptive motherhood are all subject to one fatal law: separation and loss, the only constants in her life. Both her poverty and her pride are factors in the failure to maintain either steady employment or long-term personal relationships. Other characters typically appear for several pages and then disappear, leaving Jesusa as a solitary figure of continuity in the novel. Viewed against the backdrop of this brief summary of Jesusa's life, key episodes from the text show the narrator's critical, contradictory attitudes toward her own past selves. The conflicts between the narrator and the protagonist are a function of ideological pressures that both determine her behavior and invite her determining, resisting agency.

Social class and gender are the primary ideologically charged factors that construct for Jesusa Palancares, poor and female, a position of marginality and subordination. That these forces are not monolithic in their effect on the individual is revealed in the narrator-protagonist's capacity to resist certain pressures while succumbing to others. Ample evidence for the double tendency to rebellion and conformity is to be found in the following complementary and competing dimensions of the text: the narrator's present judgments and commentary, the protagonist's past words and actions, Jesusa's relationship with the other characters that she remembers, her evocation of historical events, and, finally, the narrator's ambivalence toward speech and the act of narrating itself. A reading which pays careful attention to narrative perspective and language in the novel continually confounds any desire on our part for consistency of meaning.

Jesusa Palancares speaks and acts from within poverty and not *about* poverty. Poverty is a given in the novel, something predetermined and "natural" and therefore better seen in the details of everyday life than in explicit commentary. The need to support herself from a young age, the kinds of employment available to her, lack of housing, and the motifs of hunger and illness are the concrete ramifications of Jesusa's social class. Typically, the narrator describes these experiences in a matter-of-fact tone tinged with resignation and bitterness. She is poor among the poor, and her suffering is on a par with what she sees all around her. What does stand out is Jesusa's immense pride in her independence, a pride which can be a source of strength and an obstacle to solidarity. The need to defend herself in a hostile environment inspires both self-confidence and an extreme individualism that fosters mistrust of others. For example, in her description of a common experience among the poor, *arrimarse*, or taking shelter in another's home, Jesusa's language betrays the anger and the anxiety that lurk behind her defiant actions and her proud self-image.

> Me dormía en el suelo, detrás de un brasero, al fin que yo estaba de arrimada y tenía que acostarme en el zaguán con el perro. Dicen que el muerto y el arrimado a las veinticuatro horas apestan. Si no tenía yo dinero, ¿con qué comía? Y ¿por qué me lo habían de regalar si no tenían obligación? Harto hacían con darme el rincón, en medio de sus estrecheces. No, si no hay bondad, nadie tiene bondad, no se crea que hay bondad, no.[18]

Fiercely independent, Jesusa only moves in with another family, equally poor, as a last resort. To know herself in such need causes confusion and resentment, and the angry, critical tone of the passage conveys the protagonist's conflicting feelings of gratitude, ingratitude, humiliation, and arrogance. To be homeless means sleeping on someone else's floor with the dog, relegated to the entryway outside the human dwelling. The narrator repeats the saying about the stink of uninvited guests and dead bodies in a blow to her own dignity, but years earlier the protagonist had salvaged a measure of her pride by not additionally expecting food where she found lodging. When the narrator cuts in to deny not once but three times that there is any goodness in her benefactors, she contradicts the class solidarity that they exhibited toward her long ago. The conflict between Jesusa's pride and her need, between her individualism and her class consciousness makes her thus argue against herself in an attempt to reconcile the painful experiences of the past with her projected image of self-sufficiency. Poverty is without exception a negative and restrictive condition in the novel, which portrays human suffering as inevitable and inexplicable. The narrator-protagonist vacillates between resigned acceptance and vigorous protest against her social destiny, but in the balance, she learns that individual effort ensures survival more certainly than collective actions. The perceived failures of the Mexican Revolution, trade unionism, and a local attempt at neighborhood organizing lead Jesusa to a pessimistic disavowal of community in favor of the solitary fight for existence, which she defends in many passages in the novel.

The clearly defined gender roles into which Jesusa Palancares must fit elicit an even more complex and difficult reaction from her than do the vicissitudes of poverty. Although recognizing that social class and gender function together to influence Jesusa's behavior and discourse, I have provisionally, but not completely, separated them in my analysis. The narrator and the protagonist adopt, at different times and for different reasons, four postures toward the social construction of masculinity and femininity. On the one hand, Jesusa imitates and assimilates "masculine" behavior and correspondingly rejects many traditional feminine roles. These two postures, viewed in isolation, create for some readers the impression of her "liberated" nature. On the other hand, as active protagonist and speaking subject, Jesusa Palancares also opposes the *machismo* of her male cohorts, and on notable occasions she occupies traditionally feminine positions with skill and energy. Her idiosyncratic intervention into conventional patterns of masculine and feminine behavior stems from the conflicting demands of her personal history.

> Yo era muy hombrada y siempre me gustó jugar a la guerra, a las pedradas, a la rayuela, al trompo, a las canicas, a la lucha, a las patadas, a puras cosas de hombre, puro matar lagartijas a piedrazos, puro reventar iguanas contra las rocas. . . .
> Agujerábamos un carrizo largo y con esa cerbetana cazába-

mos: no me dolía matar a esos animalitos, ¿por qué? Todos he-
mos de morir tarde o temprano. No entiendo cómo era yo de
chica. (19–20)[19]

As a child, Jesusa is a typical tomboy, and she unquestioningly
adopts boyish pastimes and even masculine forms of violence.
The death of her mother and her dependence on her father and
older brother mean that her role models are predominantly male,
a situation that she apparently accepts as natural. Her later criticism of *machista* values, including violence against the weak,
results from many years of personal experience and does not apply to the young protagonist. For that reason the narrator disas-
sociates herself from her childish cruelty by confessing that "no
entiendo cómo era yo de chica." Similar disavowals by the narrator of her own past behavior recur throughout the novel,
conveying the emotional and ideological distance that she has
traveled.

The inclination to be "one of the boys" continues, with modi-
fications, into Jesusa's adolescent and adult years, and the image
of the narrator-protagonist as a new, liberated heroine comes
from passages like the following. "Yo no era bonita, era lo que
menos tenía y he tenido. . . . Al contrario, yo más bien quería
hacerle de hombre, alzarme las greñas, ir con los muchachos a
correr gallo, a cantar con guitarra" (70).[20] The adolescent protagonist ties up her long hair, symbol of female beauty, and
dresses as a man to go out for a good time. After her marriage,
she effects more serious role reversals by learning how to ride a
horse and shoot a rifle, disguising herself as a man in order to
accompany her husband into battle. Her adoption of male subject positions, which seems easy and uncomplicated for the child-
Jesusa, becomes increasingly untenable with age, and the mature
Jesusa combines an admiration for male freedom with a deep skepticism toward the institutions of male privilege (marriage, military, church, politics). Sexual promiscuity and violence against
women, inseparable within a system that places women in subordination to men, are the targets of the narrator's most cutting
remarks. "Los hombres son siempre abusivos. Como si eso fuera
ser hombre. Esa es la enfermedad de los mexicanos: creer que

son muy charros porque se nos montan encima" (178).[21] Therefore, despite the appeal of masculine power and liberty, Jesusa
Palancares avoids an uncritical identification with men, seeing
them as oppressors and not as models to imitate after all.

Jesusa's marriage to Pedro Aguilar is the single most important episode in her developing sense of herself as an agent as well
as an object of action. Married life in the context of the Mexican
Revolution imposes highly contradictory demands on the individual, demands which provoke unpredictable reactions. To begin with, the women who accompany the armies, whether relatively willingly as wives, girlfriends, mothers, and/or daughters
of soldiers or as unwilling captives abducted by the troops, are
thrust onto an ever-changing public stage. They usually continue
to carry out the feminine tasks of food preparation, child care, and
provision of shelter and clothing, but they perform these familiar
duties in the unfamiliar territory of highways, railroads, battle-
fields, and temporary encampments. Many women also fight in
the ranks of the revolutionary forces, and some achieve positions
of leadership.[22] Notions of feminine immobility and confinement
to the home give way before the constant mobilization of guerrilla warfare. Regional differences in dress and food often yield
to the homogeneity of the military regimen, while provincial isolation and community cohesiveness break down in contact with
a more heterogeneous population. The material and ideological
exigencies of military life may, therefore, have a liberating effect
on women such as Jesusa, who exchange the intimate world of
service to one family for the bewildering loyalties of civil war. As
portrayed in *Hasta no verte Jesús mío*, however, military marriage seems to remain true to its primary "civil" requirements in
spite of the challenging circumstances: obedience, submission,
and silence in the wife, who must be available for the service—
domestic and sexual—of her husband. The most shocking descriptions found in the novel treat Jesusa Palancares' degraded
condition as a wife:

Si de chiquilla andaba mugrosa y piojosa, con mi marido se me
agusanó la cabeza. El me pegaba, me descalabraba y con las heri-
das y la misma sangre me enllagué y se me acabó el pelo que era

largo y rizado. Allí en la cabeza estaba la plasta de mugre y allí
seguía, porque yo no me podía bañar ni me podía cambiar. (96)[23]

The young protagonist's only defense is obedient resignation
to her husband's abuse. The narrator often mentions how little
she spoke to Pedro—or to anyone—during her marriage. Her
silence faithfully duplicates the silence that she observed as a
child in other female family members. Her sister Petra was ill-
tempered and proud, but quiet and sly about hiding her feelings.
Similarly she recalls that her stepmother, Evarista Valencia,
never chatted with her or with anyone, not even her father.
When Jesusa's turn comes she follows suit, silently withstanding
Aguilar's frequent beatings. The shock value of these memories
serves to condemn masculine behavior, of course, but it can also
be read as a merciless criticism by the narrator of her former
useless and exaggerated capacity for suffering and submission:
"Así que yo fui mártir. Ora no, ora ya no soy mártir. Sufro como
todo el mundo pero no en comparación de lo que sufrí cuando
tenía marido" (97).[24]

If silence is the quintessential female condition and passivity
the married woman's only socially sanctioned defense against
male brutality, then the revolution juxtaposed the contradictory
role of combatant and the idea that the best defense is usually a
strong attack. So when Jesusa realizes that her ultimate obedience may well be an obedient death, she plots a new strategy for
survival. In one of the most exhilarating and sobering episodes
of the novel the old narrator recalls her first, decisive confrontation with her husband. After many months of abuse, Jesusa de-
cides to defend herself with stronger weapons than bent head
and stifled cries. One afternoon when Pedro orders her to accompany him away from the camp (he always beats her out of ear-
shot of the others), Jesusa hides a pistol under her blouse. Arriv-
ing at an isolated spot, "Me quedé viéndolo, *no me encogí y le
contesté*: —¿Sí? Nos matamos porque somos dos. No nomás yo
voy a morir. Saque lo suyo que yo traigo lo mío. —No sé de
dónde me entró tanto valor, yo creo que de la desesperación, y
que saco la pistola. Lueguito se asustó, vi claramente que se
asustó."[25] Neither one fires a single bullet, but the balance of

power has definitely shifted between them, and for the rest of their brief marriage Jesusa and Pedro negotiate an uneasy truce which overturns patriarchal privilege. For the first time since childhood Jesusa raises her voice to a figure of authority, and the lesson in survival that this single, daring act teaches is one that she will not forget. With a resounding *no* the protagonist refuses submission and breaks the silence barrier to affirm her individual claim to life.

What is most remarkable in the narrator's reconstruction of the episode, however, is not that she finally had the desperate courage to defend herself. Rather, the disturbing element is that, forty years later, the speaking I can express doubt as to her right to have done so: "Pero entonces yo fui la que me emperré. De por sí, yo desde chica fui mala, así nací, terrible, pero Pedro no me daba oportunidad. La bendita revolución me ayudó a desenvolverme. . . . Si yo no fuera mala me hubiera dejado de Pedro hasta que me matara. . . . Después dije que no me dejaría y cumplí la palabra. Tan no me dejé que aquí estoy" (101).[26] The narrator-protagonist never resolves her ambivalence toward the powerful weapon of language and toward her own authority as a speaking agent. Having dramatically rejected the silence of the stereotypical, long-suffering wife under the pressure of extreme danger, her later reflections on the incident give testimony to the strength of the conventions that she has momentarily refused. Self-doubt obscures a triumph won by transgressing ancient laws. During the rest of her life, the protagonist readily engages in verbal and physical duels, defending herself and others with her quick temper and tongue. Nevertheless, she doesn't forget that her deeds flagrantly violate social norms, and her voice conveys inner tensions and confusion as well as a resistant, stubborn strength.

"Después dije que no me dejaría" is a kind of declaration of independence for Jesusa with long-term implications for her marriage and her attitude toward men in general. "No dejarse," used to describe a horse that will not tolerate a saddle, also signifies a woman's resistance to domination by men. It is a fundamentally negative gesture, a refusal, and it may represent the first necessary step toward liberation for an oppressed individual or group.[27] Jesusa Palancares comes to value that refusal above all other behavior, and it defines her future interventions into society. Further, she represents her confrontation with Pedro Aguilar as an act of her individual will, the result of her unique configuration of subject positions (including orphan, tomboy, wife, *soldadera*) and not as an effect of class consciousness or any feelings of "sisterhood." Indeed, one consequence of her self-liberation is a striking lack of solidarity with other women who suffer as she did and who are not capable of the same refusal. "Yo creo que en el mismo infierno ha de haber un lugar para todas las dejadas. ¡Puros tizones en el fundillo!" (101).[28] Simply positioning oneself negatively with respect to the "feminine" brings with it the dangerous tendency to accept social conventions as inherent qualities of all women and to blame women for their oppression in a reactionary way. That is, Jesusa Palancares perceives herself to be an exception to the rule—as much natural as social in her eyes—of female submissiveness. Her comments about other women indicate her adherence to traditional notions of woman's weak, passive "nature," confirming a profound pessimism in Jesusa and allying her with patriarchal ideology against her own interests. This kind of ideological contradiction and the narrator's ambivalence toward her own survival inasmuch as it constitutes a significant challenge to social norms make of the novel an innovative and conservative document.

Many other examples could be used to illustrate the narrator-protagonist's selective inscription into male-identified roles and her rejection of normative feminine behavior. Her life-long participation in the paid labor force and her tendency to drink heavily and to fight, along with her refusal to perfect the art of making tortillas and her rejection of several marriage proposals, are exemplary behaviors. However, there are two traditional spheres of female activity and (limited) power in which Jesusa Palancares chooses to participate, but clearly on her own terms: spirituality and motherhood. The Obra Espiritual is a popular religious sect which provides a kind of empowerment to the lower class and especially to lower-class women, as Teresa González-Lee discusses in her interesting article "Jesusa Palancares, curandera espiritista o la patología de la pobreza." Having rejected the hierarchy and the hypocrisy of the Roman Catholic Church, Jesusa uses the spiritualist belief in reincarnation to make sense of her present life, and she puts her powers as a medium to practical use.[29] In one tragicomic episode she bargains with her spiritual adviser for a cure for a sick friend, arguing successfully to reduce the length of his illness from three months to two weeks. It is worth noting that in spite of her conversion, the protagonist eventually breaks with the community of the temple when she suspects that other members are trying to undermine her prestige as a successful medium. Jesusa will not allow her dignity to be compromised by those who think themselves to be superior to her. Her incursion into the Obra Espiritual does not, therefore, signify the defeat of her fighting spirit, as some interpretations suggest.[30] It is a temporary alliance with other poor women who are seeking to seize some measure of control over life and to make meaning of their experiences of suffering and exploitation.[31]

With regard to motherhood, Jesusa Palancares again occupies an idiosyncratic position. Although she never bears a child, Jesusa "mothers" three boys, whom she raises for varying periods of time. The protagonist's actions reflect responsible concern for her young charges, albeit a concern which expresses itself in both nurturance and abuse. Jesusa's violence against her adoptive sons repeats the patterns of behavior to which she was once subjected. As an additional complication, the narrator contradicts her own interest and generosity, saying time and again that she doesn't even like children. "A mí los niños nunca me han gustado. Son muy latosos y muy malas gentes" (28). "Ese muchacho se llamaba Rufino. Ya estaba grande. Era como todos los chiquillos. ¿Qué tienen de bonito? Son una calamidad andando" (239).[32] It must be admitted that all three relationships meet unfortunate ends: Angel dies, Rufino runs away and steals Jesusa's few valuables, and Perico, who lives with her the longest, also turns out to be ungrateful and a troublemaker. Jesusa narrates these calamities with her customary nonchalance, as when she describes Angel's death from pneumonia and denies feeling any sadness. But the narrator's cynicism is an imperfect shield against past and future disappointment, and she occasionally lets slip a telling remark, as when she confesses that "me quedé con tres camisitas de ese niñito Angel. Todavía las tengo" (I kept three of Angel's little shirts. I still have them) (182). Finally, Jesusa's actions in caring for these three children and in giving other kinds of assistance to many more needy youths speak loudly of her willingness to risk attachment in the face of repeated loss.

In the preceding analysis I have pried apart the close-fitted narrative pieces that construct Jesusa Palancares, and I have insisted somewhat artificially on the separation between narrator and protagonist in order to understand a fundamental contribution of *Hasta no verte Jesús mío*: the novel's portrayal of the internal contradictions within the main character, and the dynamic interaction between the individual subject and society. The discrepancies between the narrator's comments and the protagonist's actions are integral components in the novel's representation of a life lived in conflict with material and ideological limits. It is a struggle which has its moments of resignation and defeat and its moments of rebellion, all imbued with the ambivalence and stress of an uncharted journey. As a determined product of the status quo and a unique agent of discernment and contestation, Jesusa Palancares survives and narrates a story of oppression which both transcends and reaffirms the limits of individual endeavor and consciousness. The ever-shifting, everblurred boundaries between self and other, past and present, liberation and conformity are admirably recorded in the divided, enfolded I of Jesusa Palancares.

FROM TEXT TO CONTEXT: BRIDGES

Algún día que venga ya no me va a encontrar; se topará nomás con el puro viento. Llegará ese día y cuando llegue, no habrá ni quien le dé una razón. Y pensará que todo ha sido mentira. Es verdad, estamos aquí de a mentiras; . . . y mentira que me va a sentir. Si ya no le sirvo para nada, ¿qué carajos va a extrañar? Y en el taller tampoco. ¿Quién quiere usted que me extrañe si ni adioses voy a mandar? (8, epigraph to the novel)

Ahora ya no chingue. Váyase. Déjeme dormir. (316, closing lines of the novel)[33]

A dialogue is a fragile span between two supporting braces: self and other, speaker and listener, subject and object. The dialogic novel *Hasta no verte Jesús mío* rests upon its own two built-in supports, an internal frame that keeps the story from collapsing into silence. The I-narrator is one side of the bridging metaphor, her memory speaking, spanning time and space. At the opposite side, receiving the weight of words, a mute, anonymous, second person listens. You listen, for Jesusa could not maintain the flow of speech without you. You are silently present on every page, though always off to one side, out of sight. The epigraph, signed Jesusa, already constructs you/*usted* as other, visitor, friend, adversary, and the final words of the text dismiss you. In between, you are the necessary opposite pole for the narrator's highly charged message.

Like the protagonist in her moment of confrontation with Pedro Aguilar forty years earlier, the narrator of *Hasta no verte Jesús mío* chooses speech over the tempting conformity of silence. Her voice gains in momentum and authority with each anecdote that she tells until it appears that only the exhaustion of new material in the coming fusion of narrating and narrated I can put a halt to the impetus of her storytelling. But within the seemingly effortless flow of the narration, Jesusa repeatedly renounces narrative authority and laments her ineptitude at self-expression. "No tengo don de lenguas," she claims (I don't have the gift of words) (12), because she wasn't raised to be a chatterbox. Social class and gender relegate Jesusa Palancares to subordination and silence, as we have seen, and although the novel exists as proof of her defiance of social norms, it also records her many hesitations. "No puedo decir que he sido buena. Nada puedo decir" (I can't say that I have been good. I can't say anything at all) (13). Blank lines follow on the page and give pause to narrator and reader alike.

What animates the narrator to continue, besides her own pent-up emotion, that *muina* (anger) boiling inside her, is the presence of an interlocutor. Mute, nameless, and faceless, Jesusa's companion appears only as a projection of the narrator's discourse, the "you" that she evokes in hundreds of rhetorical questions and commands throughout the novel. The other is not cast as an intimate friend. The tone adopted by the narrator when she addresses her suggests that they are not of the same social class and do not share common experiences. Indeed, incomprehension, disagreement, and impatience provoke a constant shifting between reply and rebuke on Jesusa's part. The commands are mostly negative and the questions are loaded with sarcasm, as in the following passage, where Jesusa speaks bitterly of her "reunion" with the long-lost Perico and accuses her interlocutor of cruel naiveté:

> Si vino sin un centavo, jodido de cabo a rabo, ¿a qué vino? Más claro no me lo pudo decir. ¡No hombre, no sea pendeja, no se haga ilusiones! Véame a mí, a mí es a la que me da lástima cuando sale usted con su batea de babas de que la gente es buena y la quieren a uno. (313)[34]

Implicit in Jesusa's defensive posture and her frequent, scolding interruptions of the story are differences that three hundred pages of dialogue have not managed to erase. "Ahora ya no chingue. Váyase. Déjeme dormir." The text ends there, but our reading acknowledges also the encouraging energy of the repudiated interlocutor. Listening, though silent, is an act of creative intervention in dialogue, and the other side of dismissal is a meeting again, in *Hasta no verte Jesús mío*. The bridge between the narrator and her mute partner is an imperfect connection, but a connection nonetheless. In a story which vacillates between the solitude of Jesusa's individualism and the solidarity of her commitment to others, the construction of the narrative as a dialogue affirms the need for a second person to complement and complete the act of self-creation and self-salvation. The authority to speak is dictated by experience (survival) and nurtured by opportunity (dialogue): "Lo digo aunque no tengo don de lenguas, pero he atravesado muchos precipicios" (I speak even though I don't have the gift of words, but I have overcome many obstacles) (12–13). This is my own favorite penultimate version of Jesusa Palancares: a tiny, scolding figure crossing the precipice, bridging the gap between self and other—only apparently alone.

If we focus in on the figure of the listener whose mute presence animates the narrative, we find that she draws our attention across the fluid boundaries of the novel and somewhat away from Jesusa Palancares as a fictional character. The dialogue within the text thus also serves as a bridge to its context, leading the reader away from the work seen as product to an investigation of its production and its reception. This move raises a new set of issues: Elena Poniatowska's role as author of the book; the status of the text as fact (*testimonio*) or fiction (novel); the relationship between writer and informant in a project using oral testimony; and the extent to which mediating another's story involves inextricably linked acts of empowerment, betrayal, representation, and self-creation. Both Poniatowska's extensive writing about the novel and the high visibility of testimonial literature in Latin America today make such questions a logical extension of our reading of *Hasta no verte Jesús mío*, and their exploration may well offer an even more powerful critique of social relations and cultural forms than that contained in the text.

APPROXIMATIONS AND APPROPRIATIONS

Jesusa Palancares. Usted. Elena Poniatowska. Josefina Bórquez. Four linguistic signs to designate four intimately but ambiguously linked subjects in the web of writing spun in and around the novel *Hasta no verte Jesús mío*. A simple equivalence could be proposed between Jesusa Palancares and Josefina Bórquez and between the anonymous "you" and Elena Poniatowska. Reading *Hasta no verte Jesús mío* as an example of testimonial literature, problematic though that category itself is, may encourage us to look to Elena Poniatowska's friend, Josefina Bórquez, as the single "source" of the narrator-protagonist's life and language. Such a reading also places Poniatowska in the position of the interlocutor-writer, confirming the familiar pattern seen in much testimonial literature: an oral testimony given by an informant, often lower class and illiterate, to an intellectual writer-ethnographer.[35] But the inadequacy of such direct identifications soon undermines their usefulness for our interpretation of the text and its context. A closer look at the novel and at key examples of Elena Poniatowska's writing about it and about Jesusa Palancares uncovers many discrepancies and gaps that complicate the relationship between the narrative and the historical situations.

To begin, nothing in the text of *Hasta no verte Jesús mío* explicitly identifies the narrator's interlocutor ("usted") with the author, Elena Poniatowska.[36] One could conceivably read the whole book as a novel, a creation of the writer's imagination (a suggestion which in any case oversimplifies the creative process and the relationship between "fiction" and "fact"). The absence of identifying signs within *Hasta no verte Jesús mío* distances it significantly from other, more classically presented testimonial works, which build in supporting material to explain the origins of the project and to specify the "real-life" nature of their referents. The equivalent documentation for *Hasta no verte Jesús mío* must be found outside or at the margins of the novel. For example, Poniatowska's 1978 essay published in *Vuelta*, "*Hasta no verte Jesús mío*: Jesusa Palancares," provides her most frequently quoted account of meeting an argumentative old woman, "Jesusa Palancares," and writing a book based on more than a year of weekly conversations. This important essay was published in English translation in *Lives on the Line* (1988), edited by Doris Meyer.[37] But similar information had appeared as early as spring 1970 in an issue of *Vida Literaria* dedicated to articles on the recently published novel. Since then, Elena Poniatowska has referred to "Jesusa Palancares" many more times in essays and speeches, and she has answered dozens of questions about her informant's identity and their friendship, which continued long after the novel was complete. Interviews with Margarita García Flores (1982), Magdalena García Pinto (1983), and Cynthia Steele (1989) contain a wealth of material, and Poniatowska's tribute entitled "La muerte de Jesusa Palancares" (1989) carries her account of her friend's life to one kind of logical conclusion.[38]

As we read the pieces mentioned, however, we find that the abundance of material confuses more than it clarifies, opening the door to an inquiry into the status of this particular text and that of testimonial informants and authors in general. A telling example of the confusion generated by Poniatowska herself is her consistent use until the late 1980s of the name "Jesusa Palancares" to refer to both the narrator-protagonist of the novel and her real-life friend/informant. In one striking instance, an excerpt from *Hasta no verte Jesús mío* was reprinted in a 1982 issue of *fem* magazine with accompanying photos of an old peasant woman, Jesusa Palancares, presumably.[39] In a 1985 essay on the literature of La Onda in Mexico, Poniatowska blurred the conventional boundaries between fiction and fact, novel and reality, character and author even further by including Jesusa Palancares as part of La Onda and juxtaposing her name with the names of real contemporary Mexican authors such as José Agustín, Gustavo Sáinz, and Parménides García Saldaña. In the same essay, passages taken from *Hasta no verte Jesús mío* appear without citation alongside new material about Jesusa Palancares, all within the context of a report on the historical phenomenon of La Onda. Poniatowska strengthens the apparent link between what she knows to be a fictional name and extratextual reality when she describes how the protagonist of *Hasta no verte Jesús mío* acted at the funeral of "her" boss, Guillermo Gally (not himself a character in the novel but the real-life employer of Poniatowska's informant). The world of the novel and the world on which the novel is based are thus virtually indistinguishable.

The (con)fusion of character and informant is complete when Poniatowska, the essayist, asks: "What would have happened if Jesusa Palancares herself wrote her own story and I were not the author of *Hasta no verte Jesús mío?*"[40] On one level, Poniatowska is asking about the cultural politics of writing, publishing, and marketing books. What *would* it mean if an unschooled peasant woman could be an author? What changes would that effect in the traditional role of those Latin American intellectuals who choose to align themselves as spokespersons for the *pueblo*? But for the reader who "knows" all the "facts," the question also becomes a Pirandellian one of fictional characters creating themselves in search of their author/ity. The relevant facts are that Elena Poniatowska invented the name Jesusa Palancares as a mask for her friend Josefina Bórquez, who did not wish to be identified with the protagonist of *Hasta no verte Jesús mío*. In fact, Bórquez rejected the book, refusing to recognize her life in its story. Elena Poniatowska, respecting her friend's desire for privacy, could only reveal her name publicly after "Jesusa's" death in 1987. In the meantime, however, through constant use the false or fictional name had acquired a reality of its own for the book's readers and for its writer, and Elena Poniatowska continues to recall the memory of her friend-creation by invoking all her many names: Jesusa Palancares, Josefina Bórquez, Jose, Jesusa-Jose, Jose-Jesusa. The protagonist of *Hasta no verte Jesús mío* exists in so many convincing versions that she seems to live outside fiction, crossing paths with our lives and words in uncanny ways and further blurring the unstable boundaries between fiction and *testimonio*. The real-life referent, Josefina Bórquez, on the other hand, is irretrievably lost, although irresistibly attractive to readers who at times accept the too-simple equation between the character Jesusa Palancares and the informant "Jesusa Palancares." Even if we were to accept *Hasta no verte Jesús mío* as a *testimonio*, the problem of referentiality would remain. Although testimonial literature seems particularly to encourage ways of reading that posit a knowable, recoverable, historical truth, numerous recent articles question the testimonial "reality effect" without denying the importance of its impact on the reader.[41]

Poniatowska's borderline writing frequently poses a challenge to systems of textual classification, and two recent articles thoughtfully and carefully approach the question of the genre of *Hasta no verte Jesús mío*. María Inés Lagos-Pope borrows a phrase from the publicity blurb printed on the back cover of many editions of the novel as a useful handle for her fine analysis of the book as a *testimonio creativo*. My comments above show that I would agree with Lagos-Pope's thesis that *Hasta no verte Jesús mío* combines strategies of novelistic and testimonial writing to produce a hybrid form that challenges hegemonic discourse. Lucille Kerr also effectively problematizes any attempt at easy categorization of the book in her essay "Gestures of Authorship: Lying to Tell the Truth." Both critics read the novel in the context of Latin American *testimonio* and mindful of Elena Poniatowska's other writings, and their analyses have broad implications for reading in general. Kerr suggests that all testimonial literature pushes us to ask how *any* given text becomes accepted as truthful, convincingly arguing out many of the sources of confusion that I have reviewed above. While I have questions about Kerr's use of *Hasta no verte Jesús mío* as an "exemplary but not representative" (370) work of testimonial literature, her analysis of the structures of truth and lies and their relation to the elusive real is extremely interesting. Certainly a crucial strategy in the testimonial critique of hegemonic versions of history is its appeal to our sense of the true, even if, as Kerr shows for *Hasta no verte Jesús mío*, what we get is not the true but the "convincingly verisimilar," a "persuasive lie."[42] The studies by Lagos-Pope and Kerr make significant contributions to the debate over *Hasta no verte Jesús mío*. In the following analysis of approximations and appropriations in the production of the text, I open up new intertextual space to explore the ethical dilemmas—and opportunities—posed by the project.

There are certain constants in Elena Poniatowska's numerous retellings of how she met Josefina Bórquez. The writer recalls that she once overheard an old woman arguing with someone in a laundry and then encountered her again in jail. Attracted by the woman's extraordinary language and her remarkably combative tone, Poniatowska searched her out to ask if she could visit her and talk with her. Josefina Bórquez initially rejected Elena Poniatowska's overtures, saying that she had to work and she didn't have time to sit and chat, but she ultimately consented to regular Wednesday afternoon visits. The now familiar story of their weekly conversations and their developing friendship, which began in 1963, is one of refusal and acceptance, silence and communication across the lines of class and generation difference, as Poniatowska herself testifies. "Grudgingly, Jesusa agreed to my seeing her on the only day of the week she had free: Wednesday, from four to six. I began to live a little from Wednesday to Wednesday. Jesusa, on the other hand, did not give up her hostile attitude" ("Here's to You," 140). Elena Poniatowska's matter-of-fact tone in this statement and in others masks an important point: the highly improbable nature of any such encounter and friendship between a wealthy Mexican professional woman and a peasant woman outside the household circle. In spite of the writer's low-key presentation of what she herself has called the fundamental meeting of her life, it would be a mistake to take for granted Poniatowska's attention to Josefina Bórquez's language. I believe that we can begin to appreciate just how unlikely an event it was, and why Elena Poniatowska was uniquely capable of participating in it, by turning to the essays of French philosopher Simone Weil. Generally overlooked in the existing criticism on Elena Poniatowska, the biography and the writings of Simone Weil have exerted a decisive influence on the Mexican writer's social thought. Poniatowska has mentioned her name in a number of published interviews, and Weil figures prominently along with "Jesusa Palancares" in one of Poniatowska's most important essays: her lengthy introduction to Ana Gutiérrez's testimonial project on Peruvian domestic workers, *Se necesita muchacha*. Simone Weil's writing provides crucial insights into the meaning of Poniatowska's oft-celebrated capacity to hear and to *heed* the voices of the oppressed.

In the essay "Human Personality," written in the last year of her brief life, Simone Weil formulated her thoughts on oppression, privilege, good intentions, and the articulation of suffering by the afflicted. Referring to the deadening, silencing effect of "affliction" (her term), she wrote that "even in those who still have the power to cry out, the cry hardly ever expresses itself, either inwardly or outwardly, in *coherent language*."[43] "Affliction is by its nature inarticulate," and when the silent are given words by others these words are usually ill-chosen "because those [the privileged] who choose them know nothing of the affliction they would interpret." And why is this so? "Thought revolts from contemplating affliction, to the same degree that living flesh recoils from death. A stag advancing voluntarily step by step to offer itself to the teeth of a pack of hounds is about as probable as an act of attention directed towards a real affliction, which is close at hand, on the part of a mind which is free to avoid it."[44]

The image of the stag going willingly to its death is a powerful metaphor for the barriers to communication that exist between those who suffer and those who are "free to avoid it." Weil's words echo in Elena Poniatowska's accounts of meeting Josefina

Bórquez and writing *Hasta no verte Jesús mío*. Consider the following comments, made by Poniatowska in 1970, which attest to the improbability of a conscious "act of attention" to affliction on the part of a privileged member of society.

> Jesusa existe, es cierto. Es un ser de carne y hueso. Un personaje vivo . . . Para los demás, Jesusa es una pobre vieja que repite hasta la saciedad cosas extrañas—, muchas veces tediosas. . . . Quéjese y quéjese, Jesusa es igual a un montón de viejos; de esos que van caminando por la banqueta, pegados a la pared y *de quienes uno se aparta instintivamente porque entorpecen nuestro paso*, y siempre tenemos prisa."[45]

Elena Poniatowska thus testifies to the novel's basis in conversations with a real "Jesusa," and she confirms Weil's observations about the revulsion felt by the privileged toward the afflicted. Aversion to suffering is a frequently occurring theme in Elena Poniatowska's essays, where she puzzles out our easy sympathy for far-off misery and our disgust before the familiar faces of pain. What she doesn't address, but which concerns us here, is her own capacity to attend to the Jesusas of Mexico and to listen to their strange, tedious stories with interest and respect.

The philosophy of Simone Weil undoubtedly has stimulated Elena Poniatowska's perception of the harm done to the poor of Mexico and Latin America by the multiple oppressions that they suffer. Poniatowska's formal schooling was notoriously deficient in intellectual terms, and her independent reading of books in French, Spanish, and English, along with her experience as a journalist, comprise the best part of her education. Books found in her parents' home, books recommended by mentors, books which now arrive from all over the world and flood her personal library are teachers and companions to which she may return time and again. So it has been with the biography and the essays of Simone Weil, whose disinterested activism and capacity for self-sacrifice Poniatowska greatly admires. But the ideas absorbed through reading are only one factor in Elena Poniatowska's formation that played a key role in her serendipitous 1963 encounter with Josefina Bórquez. Many of the details of the writer's childhood and upbringing also prepared her for hearing the other's muffled voice. Poniatowska's deeply felt need to belong to Mexico and to establish roots in contradiction to her family heritage of privileged vagabondage has always been a compelling force in her personal relationships and her work. As a child, abruptly uprooted from France to Mexico, she formed close emotional bonds with her Mexican nanny, Magdalena Castillo, and with her family's other domestic servants. Indigenous or *mestiza* women, recently displaced from the countryside to the urban environment, Magdalena Castillo and her cohorts taught Elena Poniatowska her first Spanish, their own popular Mexican Spanish with its grammatical deviations and regional vocabulary. These bonds—emotional and linguistic—have trained Elena Poniatowska's ear to detect familiar, telling tones in voices that others hear only as noise, nuisance, or nothing.

Simone Weil's passionately held political and religious convictions led her to renounce the material benefits of her social class and professional status and to share as closely as possible the experiences and the suffering of the poor. Many people view her choice as excessively, incomprehensibly self-denying, almost suicidal. Clearly, in spite of her admiration for Weil's philosophy of solidarity, Elena Poniatowska has made a different set of choices. Rather than abandon one world for another, Poniatowska lives between worlds, struggling to keep her balance between her witness to injustice and her own comfortable level of existence. She is acutely aware of the tensions and the contradictions that surround her person and her work in the patriarchal, class-based structure of Mexican society, and the imperative to confront difference marks her writing of *Hasta no verte Jesús mío* and her later meditations on that work.[46] And so, while the philosophical writings of Simone Weil opened the door for our consideration of the moral dimensions of Elena Poniatowska's writing, they leave unaddressed many aspects of the ethical and political dilemma inherent in the Mexican author's attempt to "give voice" to the historically silenced other.

In the following pages I conclude my study of *Hasta no verte Jesús mío* by further examining the production of the text in the light of recent feminist ethnographic theory. The concerns that

Poniatowska expresses and the results of her writing process are similar in some respects to the dilemmas articulated by North American feminist ethnographers, particularly those who interview nonelite subjects across class and cultural lines. The 1991 volume entitled *Women's Words: The Feminist Practice of Oral History* includes important essays by Judith Stacey and Daphne Patai which prove to be particularly helpful in detecting the twists and turns of the ethical labyrinth.

In the essay "Can There Be a Feminist Ethnography?" sociologist Judith Stacey measures her experiences in conducting oral history interviews with women against feminist research principles and theories of postmodern ethnography. Her self-critique shows that her initial enthusiasm for a "face-to-face research experience"[47] soon ceded to considerable anxiety over the contradictions inherent in positioning oneself as both researcher and friend, observer and participant, ethnographer and feminist, authority and collaborator in other women's lives. Finding the tensions between professional and personal responsibilities and between benefit and loss to researcher and subject alike to be finally irreconcilable, Stacey outlines no solutions to the ethical conundrum, although she does reaffirm the need for a continuing dialogue between feminists and ethnographers.

Daphne Patai's work among Brazilian women in the early 1980s leads her to ask "Is Ethical Research Possible?" and to conclude that it is not, at least not in an absolute sense. For Patai, the systemic material inequalities between a First World researcher and a nonelite Third World subject force her to shift attention from ethical considerations to the political dimensions of conducting research on/with oppressed subjects. Both Stacey and Patai, like Poniatowska, set out to create opportunities for responsible, positive action on behalf of women, only to find themselves confronting ethical dilemmas and contradictions that often put them directly at odds with their informants and at odds with their own feminist principles. The fact of research as an intrusion that may upset a person's life, the hierarchical nature of many supposedly collaborative efforts, the possibility for betrayal and exploitation of the informant, the danger of seeing their respect for the informant lead to a distortion of data (as in excluding sensitive information), and the researcher's freedom to leave behind the conditions of life within which the informant must remain are among the problems that Stacey and Patai discuss and that Elena Poniatowska also confronts.

However, it bears repeating, when evoking the authority of sociologists and anthropologists, that *Hasta no verte Jesús mío* is not structured like other well-known pieces of testimonial literature, and it cannot be considered an ethnographic or anthropological study per se. Absent from the text itself is the documentation that explains the author's intentions and creates a pact with the reader to accept the book as a true account of historical events and persons. There are no photographs of Jesusa Palancares, no maps, no tables, no historical chronology, no footnotes: none of the factual support usually provided to strengthen the testimonial claim to authenticity. Significantly, some of what sets the book apart from *testimonio* resulted from factors beyond the author's control. That is, left to her own devices, Elena Poniatowska may well have produced a more conventionally configured testimonial text. For example, she had planned to write an introduction, use the name of Josefina Bórquez, and include photographs of her, but two parties intervened to censure these plans. Josefina Bórquez herself refused to authorize the use of her name and photographs, an exercise of her limited power to control the process and to control access to her person. The editor of the book at the publishing house preferred to issue it without the proposed introduction so that it would appear more like a conventional novel. Thus, both respect for the informant's desires and market forces heavily influenced the form of the published text. "Testimonial novel" and *testimonio creativo*, with an emphasis on "novel" and "*creativo*," are therefore suitable labels if we must choose one.

However, the reading public's expectations of Elena Poniatowska as a journalist and its preconceptions about testimonial literature have led to much confusion over the production of the text. For example, Poniatowska has been asked repeatedly about her use of a tape recorder in her weekly sessions with Josefina Bórquez. The tape recorder is the primary technology behind most oral history projects, but Elena Poniatowska has explained that she used it very little due to Josefina Bórquez's opposition. Taking notes by hand during their interviews also apparently disrupted the dialogue, because Bórquez grew impatient with interruptions or delays, so at some point Poniatowska began to wait until she returned home in the evening to reconstruct on paper the afternoon's conversation.[48] Even granting that all oral history involves selection and interpretation by the researcher, Elena Poniatowska's procedure clearly implies an especially high degree of filtering and mediation of the informant's words. In addition, Elena Poniatowska invented episodes and characters to suit her interests and the book's overall scheme. In recreating Josefina Bórquez's story, the writer downplayed some of her informant's favorite topics, including the Obra Espiritual and her constant complaints about the deterioration of living conditions in Mexico City. Finally, the protagonist's language is not strictly that of Bórquez but a synthesis of colloquial Spanish absorbed from a number of different speakers and recreated by the writer.[49] All these interventions constitute a substantial fictionalization of Josefina Bórquez's version of events—itself already a constructed narrative and no simple reflection of experience.

In spite of the preceding disclaimers, important aspects of the whole process of writing *Hasta no verte Jesús mío* do link Poniatowska's efforts with the work of ethnographers like Judith Stacey and Daphne Patai. As a writer living and working in the interstices of class and ethnic divisions, Elena Poniatowska has faced the same dangers that they so courageously acknowledge, and her own reflections on testimonial literature, on *Hasta no verte Jesús mío*, and on her relationship with Josefina Bórquez illustrate common dilemmas. I have translated the following passage from "Literatura testimonial," a manuscript based on a series of lectures that the author delivered in Germany in 1984.[50]

An ethical problem arises around the writing of testimonial novels. Are those who create them writers or not? Are they simply opportunists who . . . plunge into the manufacture of easily consumed works that will fill the void between the elite and the illiterate in Latin American countries? . . . They confiscate a reality, present it as their own, steal their informants' words, plagiarize their colloquialisms, tape their language and take possession of their very souls.[51]

Here Elena Poniatowska uses rhetorical questions and negatively charged vocabulary to an ironic effect in subverting certain assumptions about testimonial literature that she perceived among her European audiences in 1984. Her target was the tendency, perhaps more widespread then than now, to privilege "pure" literature over nonfiction and testimonial works. Poniatowska grounds her defense of *testimonio* on the political and cultural importance of writing about the "people without history" in societies built upon extremes of wealth, misery, privilege, and oppression. Poniatowska further acknowledges that such writing often confronts readers who are hostile to the "truths of their own reality,"[52] while at the same time she points out the real potential for abuse of the testimonial subject. However, due to the primarily defensive posture that she adopts, "Literatura testimonial" finally offers a rather simplistic vision of the production of testimonial texts. Poniatowska unsatisfactorily resolves the ironically posed questions of responsibility, appropriation, and social difference by appealing later in the paper to the inherent authenticity of the narratives discussed and the good intentions of their authors. She suggests that nonelite speakers ("personajes populares") possess a voice which is somehow natural, true, and authentic to experience, powerful because free from "formalisms." This kind of essentialism contradicts the emphasis on the social construction of culture and discourse (or voice) which complicates Stacey's and Patai's arguments. Indeed, one of the dangers of testimonial literature is that the sense of political and historical urgency which it conveys may induce us to overlook the problematic nature of its representation of "other voices." In this regard, Gayatri Chakravorty Spivak's warning that the subaltern woman remains *mute* even in the most radical intellectual's "representation" of her forces a reevaluation of notions of authenticity in discourse.[53] It is not my aim here to look for a coherent theory of testimonial literature in Elena Poniatowska's essays nor to imply that she ought to provide us with one. Rather, I refer to these texts for insights—provisional and incomplete—into her writing process. I have found that the essays dealing specifically with *Hasta no verte Jesús mío* and her friendship with Josefina Bórquez/Jesusa Palancares contain subtle, searching deliberations into her sense of guilt over her failure to represent Josefina Bórquez adequately, the disproportionate benefit accruing to the writer of *testimonio*, the inevitable separation between writer and informant once the book was complete, and, in general, the necessarily hierarchical relationship that exists between women of different social classes.

> I feel that I didn't do her [Josefina Bórquez] justice with *Hasta no verte Jesús mío*; I obeyed her, faithful to the point of exacerbation, hanging on each of her gestures like a person in love. . . . I had the feeling that I was stealing her words and that, in exchange for the treasure that she was unknowingly placing in my hands, I would not even be able to offer a portrait of her essence. No one on earth has given me what Jesusa offered me . . . that's how testimonial literature is. It fills one with anxiety, with insecurity. One handles very fragile material, people's hearts; their names, which are their honor; their work; and their time.[54]

The autobiographical essay "A Question Mark Engraved on My Eyelids," quoted above, contains one of many tributes by Elena Poniatowska to the benefits that she received from knowing Josefina Bórquez. The writer perceives that her friend's words, her time, and even her name were precious gifts that the author struggled unsuccessfully to repay by creating a story worthy of her generosity. One of the principal benefits derived by Poniatowska and by all writers who are in a similar position is the publication of a book under their own name. Professional status, potential royalties, and in Poniatowska's case a prestigious literary prize belong to the "author" of the text as defined by copyright convention and law. So it is that we accept as natural that Elena Poniatowska won the 1970 Premio Mazatlán de Literatura for *Hasta no verte Jesús mío* at the same time that we recognize the book's testimonial qualities.

Elena Poniatowska has also spoken of less tangible gifts received from Josefina Bórquez. The writer's national and cultural identity grew much stronger in contact with this untypical representative of the Mexican *pueblo*, and she feels that Bórquez's acceptance of her was an important moment in her desire to belong to Mexico. "Writing to belong" is a leitmotif of Poniatowska's reflections on her work, and Josefina Bórquez held the power to validate her fragile sense of *mexicanidad* by providing a way to partially overcome the formidable class barriers that separate "una niña de bien" like Poniatowska from the majority of Mexican citizens. Little by little in the course of interviewing Bórquez and reconstructing the interviews at home, Elena Poniatowska began to feel that "Mexico was inside me; . . . One night before falling asleep and after identifying myself for a long time with Jesusa, reviewing all my images of her one by one, I was able to tell myself in a whisper: 'I *do* belong'" ("Here's to You," 147).

Elena Poniatowska also began to accept herself as a woman and to celebrate female strengths and female rebellion in the presence of Josefina Bórquez's defiant, combative spirit. "Because of her I also love being a woman, I who, at age fifteen, wanted to be a man."[55] These comments make it clear that the process of knowing and representing the other is inseparable from representing the self, and indeed self-creation may take precedence when the other is unable to speak directly on her own behalf. "Jesusa Palancares" is the name given to this process of other-oriented self-knowledge in Elena Poniatowska's life. The invented name denominates not only a character in a novel but is also the verbal sign of a constant presence in the writer's imagination, a kind of touchstone, as is Simone Weil, for Poniatowska's social and political thought. Elena Poniatowska returns over and over to Jesusa Palancares' words, now praising "her" strength, now criticizing "her" solitary individualism, and always, I would suggest, subjecting *herself* to scrutiny.

The relative benefit or loss experienced by her friend, on the contrary, is impossible to assess, as the records pertaining to their relationship belong to Elena Poniatowska. Josefina Bórquez's culturally determined silence and invisibility is an inescapable fact in spite of Poniatowska's efforts to communicate her story, and Poniatowska herself raises doubts about what Bórquez "got" out of their friendship and the book. Certainly the efforts adopted by some researchers to "return the research to the community" and to encourage active collaboration in the production of the text do not apply to a book like *Hasta no verte Jesús mío*, which Poniatowska wrote from her notes during a year's stay in France. In any case Daphne Patai convincingly explodes the idea that such gestures go very far in correcting the material and symbolic imbalances that exist in the research situation.[56] With characteristic expressions of guilt, Poniatowska admits that she was unable to offer anything to Josefina Bórquez that could improve her desolate condition or match her informant's impact on the writer's life. If Bórquez accepted a gift from her, it was only to wrap it up and put it away, never to use or enjoy it. Invitations to revisit Bórquez's home town met with stubborn refusal, leaving Poniatowska to conclude that either the habit of suffering was too deeply ingrained in her friend or else she herself was at fault for not knowing how to convince her. One inevitable loss experienced (unequally) in these situations is the eventual abandonment of the subject of the testimony by the writer or researcher. This abandonment is, ironically, made more acute by the very effort to develop intimacy and mutual respect that feminists celebrate. According to Elena Poniatowska, Josefina Bórquez accurately predicted the moment of loss, accusing her in advance of interested motivations for the visits. "You and your self-centered interest! You'll keep coming to see me as long as you can get something out of me that benefits you, and afterwards not a trace, not even your taillights" ("Here's to You," 150). In a later interview Poniatowska confesses that "I feel very bad because later I stopped seeing her so much. After all we didn't see eye to eye. After a while I didn't make the effort to go to see her."[57]

My point is not to suggest that guilt and remorse are appropriate responses to the dilemmas that an unethical, unequally structured world presents to us. In fact, I agree with Daphne Patai that neither apologizing for privilege nor ignoring it is a responsible reaction to the political implications of work like hers or like Elena Poniatowska's. Nor do I wish to deny the positive value that both women derived from their long-lasting friendship and from the trust that grew between them. Rather, I see Poniatowska's persistent attempts over the course of more than twenty years to explain her bond to Josefina Bórquez and, in a sense, to pay her debt to her as a valuable contribution to understanding the potential and the limits of testimonial production and of any attempt by the elite to represent the subaltern other. By reading Elena Poniatowska's reflections on *Hasta no verte Jesús mío* along with the text, we can appreciate the combination of empowerment (giving voice) and appropriation (taking interpretive control of the other's voice) entailed by such a project, and we may avoid accepting the illusion that the nonelite, nonliterate woman has either spoken to us or has been given back a voice that is unproblematically true to her consciousness. To return in concluding to the analysis of narrative voice and subjectivity, one of the achievements of the "writings" of/on *Hasta no verte Jesús mío* is the presentation of the narrator/protagonist/informant as a divided and not finally comprehensible subject of speech and action, a human agent who reserves as many mysteries as she reveals and who has a role in deciding when to open the door to the intrusive other and when to barricade it against her. "Ahora ya no chingue. Váyase. Déjeme dormir."

Elena Poniatowska is profoundly disturbed by the world in which she lives, and as a writer she knows herself to be uniquely authorized to speak in and about that world. The writing of *Hasta no verte Jesús mío* was a crucial moment in her engagement with Mexican society, a hinge between past and future, between not belonging and belonging, between observation of and participation in her nation's life. Her continued commitment to denouncing injustice is tempered by an acute awareness of the imperfect interpretive capacity of any one person and the limited power of any single text to affect institutions or individuals. Poniatowska has said that in the company of Josefina Bórquez she experienced genuine, insurmountable poverty on its own terms for the first time. Her repeated references to that experience show a shift from a primarily personal, intimate view of suffering to an understanding of social class conflicts and structural inequalities. In "Presentación al lector mexicano," her long essay on domestic workers which I mentioned earlier, Elena Poniatowska brings together disparate elements of autobiography, philosophy, sociology, and feminism in a probing analysis of the patron-servant relationship. This essay, written in 1981, particularly focuses on the contradictions that Poniatowska constantly—and only partially successfully—negotiates on a day-to-day basis. She examines the tensions between intimacy and distance, egotism and generosity, good intentions and failed communication, concluding that purely individual efforts will never eliminate the conditions upon which social divisions rest. "We can't, as individuals, throw our little personal bridges across the immense abyss of which Domitila Barrios speaks. Like it or not, class struggle is here to stay, it is a fact of life, and my efforts seem more like illusions, impossible dreams, than real solutions." [58] In the decade preceding and in the decade following those remarks, works like *Hasta no verte Jesús mío*, *La noche de Tlatelolco*, *Fuerte es el silencio*, and *Nada, nadie* attest to Poniatowska's indefatigable determination to act responsibly and in solidarity with others to "find the words which express the truth of their affliction." [59] To her immense credit, Elena Poniatowska's most significant efforts to "give voice" to the oppressed are finally suffused with the poignant recognition that such truths are always partial, ideologically charged versions of others—and of ourselves.

CHRONICLES OF THE CONQUERED

*Authority and History in
'La noche de Tlatelolco'*

A borderline text like *Hasta no verte Jesús mío* and Elena Poniatowska's continuing reflections on the book and on her friendship with Josefina Bórquez lay bare the inevitable tensions between empowerment and appropriation of the other's voice in testimonial modes of literature. Both Poniatowska's essays and her readers' analyses of the "creative confusions" generated by that tension make it impossible to accept at face value a deceptively simple statement like the following: "My interest in writing is simply to give a voice to those who don't have one."[1] As we have seen, the "giving" of discursive authority and the "recording" of other voices are politically and ideologically charged events, excursions into an explosive territory which must be approached with respect and care. Elena Poniatowska's oft-acknowledged commitment to negotiating the minefields of silence, memory, and dialogue has led her to produce many other contestatory versions of national life in contemporary Mexico. In the process, she willingly and repeatedly engages with the problematical "gestures of authorship" (see Lucille Kerr), creating new solutions to long-standing problems of representation. The student movement of 1968, the aftermath of the 1985 earthquake in Mexico City, the experience of female domestic workers, a squatters' colony and its destruction by the Mexican government: these are only a few of the complex stories that Elena Poniatowska has investigated and made public in texts such as *La noche de Tlatelolco, Fuerte es el silencio*, and *Nada, nadie: Las voces del temblor*. Further, these books constitute a significant contribution to the burgeoning corpus of Latin American testimonial discourse of the past twenty-five years, linking Poniatowska across national boundaries with the work and the aspirations of other writers.

Throughout Latin America, events of the past three decades have created both the need and the conditions for the writing of what is commonly referred to as *testimonio*, or testimonial literature.[2] As I use the term here, *testimonio* denominates a broad, flexible category of nonfiction texts which record contemporary events from the perspective of direct participants or witnesses.[3] The subjects of the events may "author" their own written account, as did Alicia Partnoy in her book about Argentina's "dirty war," *The Little School: Tales of Disappearance and Survival in Argentina*. Or the subjects, for reasons of illiteracy or lack of access to the means of publication, may work in collaboration with a professional writer, often a journalist, anthropologist, ethnographer, or sociologist. Miguel Barnet's *Biografía de un cimarrón* (1966; *Autobiography of a Runaway Slave*, 1966) and Rigoberta Menchú and Elisabeth Burgos Debray's *Me llamo Rigoberta Menchú y así me nació la conciencia* (1983; *I, Rigoberta Menchú*, 1984) are two of the best-known examples of the latter, collaborative process.[4] However it is produced, most testimonial literature shares an explicit commitment to denounce repression and abuse of authority, raise the consciousness of its readers about situations of political, economic, and cultural terror, and offer an alternative view to official, hegemonic history. As such, it necessarily foregrounds issues of power, powerlessness, resistance, and subversion in the interconnected discourses of politics, history, and literature.

As a journalist working in the capital city, Elena Poniatowska has enjoyed privileged access to the people and events of the past thirty-five years of Mexican history. In chapter 1, I showed how her early work as an interviewer introduced her to the "great men" of Mexico and Spanish America in a context that tended to highlight their power and prestige to the detriment of Poniatowska's agency as a speaking subject. Dialogue negotiated from a position of gender, social, and cultural subordination offered limited opportunities to challenge authority, although in their conversations with the "naive," "ignorant" young journalist, the interviewees may have betrayed more than they intended about their own investment in the status quo.

Elena Poniatowska, for her part, entered the mainstream of Mexican culture through the side door of society news and the journalistic interview. In the ten years following the publication of *Palabras cruzadas*, a variety of factors combined to broaden and sharpen Poniatowska's perceptions of the vast, unequally configured human landscape of Mexico. The influence of intellectuals who served as mentors, her own active engagement with the protagonists of both newsworthy events and "everyday life," and the crucial meetings with Josefina Bórquez encouraged the writer's growing awareness of the structural inequities that distort the life of her nation. Class divisions, economic exploitation, gender inequality, and political repression are dominant concerns in the books mentioned and in other writings such as *Gaby Brimmer* and the short stories of *De noche vienes*. Both formal interviews and less structured conversations with people of all social backgrounds and political orientations provide the multiple perspectives against which the writer can measure and interpret her personal experiences and her wide-ranging reading in the direction of an increasingly critical view of Mexican society.

The first project in which Elena Poniatowska elaborates a documentary, although emphatically not a *testimonial*, approach to depicting the life of the poor is the collaboratively conceived and executed *Todo empezó el domingo* (1963), a text whose writing antedates her friendship with Josefina Bórquez. Poniatowska credits fellow journalist and illustrator Alberto Beltrán with the idea for *Todo empezó el domingo*, which is a collection of sixty-three short *costumbrista* articles written by Poniatowska and illustrated by Beltrán. They treat the customs, Sunday pastimes, and daily haunts of the lower middle class and popular sectors in Mexico City and in provincial towns. Many of the vignettes describe such entertainments as Sunday afternoon soccer games, religious processions, dances, the matinée at the cinema, public baths, and free open-air concerts. Others focus on a public building or a geographical location like Chapultepec Park, Chichén Itzá, or the Torre Latinoamericana in order to explore Mexican history and establish links between modern Mexico and its indigenous past. A recurrent theme is the critique of tourism and the disparity between wealthy tourists and the impoverished human objects of their sight-seeing excursions. Finally, a third group of articles exposes corruption, economic exploitation, and U.S. involvement in Mexican industry by denouncing the abuse of child labor, the military draft, the mining industry, and miserable prison conditions.

The predominant tone of *Todo empezó el domingo*, however, even in the articles marked by social protest, conveys a *costumbrista* delight in the attractiveness of the "popular." The narrator provides an abundance of colorful detail, and she imitates popular forms of speech in her evocation of the suffering but ultimately picturesque *pueblo*. In addition, the narrator is always positioned as a distant observer who watches and overhears the *pueblo* ("them"), sentimentalizing her subject matter in the process. There are occasional self-conscious moments when she acknowledges her own status as a kind of tourist among the masses, but on the whole *Todo empezó el domingo* represents a very tentative encounter between the writer and her social and economic other, an encounter which does little to examine the gap between the upper-class reporter and her less privileged subjects. And so, even while leaving behind the world of the elite addressed in *Palabras cruzadas*, *Todo empezó el domingo* manages to view the anonymous, faceless multitude from a safe distance.

In *Hasta no verte Jesús mío* Elena Poniatowska clearly moved far beyond the *costumbrismo* of *Todo empezó el domingo*, and she has made important contributions to testimonial literature with two collectively voiced oral histories: *Nada, nadie: Las voces del temblor*, a loosely structured account of the 1985 earthquake in Mexico City and its aftermath, and *La noche de Tlatelolco*, her widely known chronicle of the 1968 Mexican student movement. In both books Poniatowska gathers and edits oral testimonies, newspaper articles, and photographs to create a montage of heterogeneous discourses about a complex series of interrelated events. The individual testimonies provide the largest source of material in both cases, and Poniatowska took notes or, less often, taped her informants' stories for later compilation into the published form.

The two texts voice a chilling denunciation of government corruption and violence—whether it be the violence of guns in 1968 or the violence of grossly mismanaged disaster relief in 1985. *Nada, nadie* was first published as a series of daily articles in 1985 in the leftist newspaper *La Jornada* after Poniatowska's long-time employer, *Novedades*, refused to accept them. "I began to turn them off at *Novedades*, so much so that they told me not to give them the articles because, I believe, they had received an order from the government. They told me, 'No more! It depresses people terribly.' . . . That day I had my article in my hand, *La Jornada* was close by, and I went over there."[5] Self-censorship by the newspaper because of commercial concerns and possible direct government interference prevented an establishment newspaper like *Novedades* from continuing to publish the disturbing news of human suffering, civilian solidarity, and official corruption and ineptitude that *Nada, nadie* documents. For Elena Poniatowska writing in Mexico, an alternative channel for publication was not difficult to locate, but her experience recalls the many barriers that authors of *testimonios* working in other countries or on other topics may face in retrieving and disseminating stories which run counter to officially sanctioned discourse.[6]

The chronicles of *Fuerte es el silencio* represent another kind of documentary text which Elena Poniatowska has cultivated as a logical extension of her journalism. *Fuerte es el silencio* brings together five separate pieces which treat specific situations of repression and poverty and the people or groups that have taken up the struggle against them. The topics of the articles are the 1968 student movement, political prisoners, a hunger strike by mothers of disappeared persons, a squatters' colony, and the plight of the hundreds of thousands of impoverished peasants who settle each year in the slums that encircle Mexico City. In two of the chronicles individual protagonists stand out against the backdrop of their anonymous followers. In "Diario de una huelga de hambre" (Diary of a hunger strike) Poniatowska singles out her friend Rosario Ibarra de la Piedra, a human rights activist on behalf of the disappeared and a candidate for the presidency of Mexico in 1982. "La colonia Rubén Jaramillo" (The Rubén Jaramillo settlement) offers a fictionalized portrayal of Florencio ("El Güero") Medrano, the visionary leader of the aforementioned *colonia*, a socialist farming cooperative organized in 1973 on "invaded" lands in Cuernavaca. The silence commemorated by the book's title and breached by the book's contents is the killing silence imposed on political dissidents, women, and the poor in Mexico. Equally a target of Poniatowska's critique is the complicitous silence of private business, the press, and the citizenry in general before the glaring inequities of social and economic injustice and an abusive power structure.

Poniatowska's research for writing the five chronicles involved interviews as well as investigation of such public records as Amnesty International reports, census documents, sociological studies, and the press. One intriguing aspect of these articles which Cynthia Steele has addressed in a recent essay is the way in which Elena Poniatowska has written herself into *Fuerte es el silencio* in more overt forms than she assumes in the oral history *La noche de Tlatelolco* or the testimonial novel *Hasta no verte Jesús mío*.[7] Poniatowska's highlighted presence as a reporter or as a (thinly) fictionalized character in the chronicles reveals the conflicting sentiments of guilt, responsibility, sympathy, solidarity, outrage, unease, and exhaustion that characterize the writer's critical and self-critical commitment to combatting the deafening silence of society's Juans and Marías. Like Simone Weil in the Europe of the 1930s, Poniatowska insists that her readers attend to the nameless "nobodys" who are everywhere to be seen, but rarely heard, by those of us privileged to write and consume books. "'Pues póngale nomás Juan' como si con dar su nombre temieran molestar, ocupar un sitio en el espacio y el tiempo que no les corresponde, 'nomás Juan' . . . Si la mayoría sólo existe de bulto (es 'el pueblo') los pobres no tienen voz. Fuerte es su silencio."[8]

Elena Poniatowska's most significant achievement in nonfiction writing is *La noche de Tlatelolco: Testimonios de historia oral.* 1968 was a year of opportunity and crisis for Mexico. After forty years in power, the government of the ruling Institutional Revolutionary Party (PRI), headed by President Gustavo Díaz Ordaz, was anxious to demonstrate to the world that Mexico was not the underdeveloped, violence-prone country populated by the gun-toting bandits and lazy peasants of Hollywood movie sets. The summer Olympic Games, scheduled for October 12–27 in Mexico City, were planned as a showcase for modernization and stable democracy in an economically developing nation. At the same time, growing political dissidence in Mexico challenged the monolithic state apparatus and the power monopoly of the PRI.

The betrayal of the 1910 revolution and dissatisfaction with the government and its economic policies have been constant themes of Mexican literature since the 1920s, and opposition by intellectuals to the status quo was therefore not a phenomenon unique to the 1960s. But by 1968, a decade of repressive measures taken by the government against labor activists, teachers, and university students and the atmosphere of student rebellion in Europe and the United States combined to create a critical juncture in Mexican history. It was at this moment, virtually on the eve of the Olympics, when international attention would be focused on the country, that a series of initially spontaneous incidents aroused the students of the Universidad Nacional Autónoma de México (UNAM) and the Instituto Politécnico Nacional (IPN) into organizing what came to be known as the Movimiento Estudiantil, the 1968 Mexican student movement.

A brief summary of the events of late July through October 1968 must begin by acknowledging that the initial confrontations between the students and the police had nothing to do with strikes or demands for political reforms. On July 22 a street fight among students of secondary schools associated with the IPN and the UNAM escalated when riot police intervened. The resulting conflict motivated a public demonstration against police violence on July 26, the same day that several leftist associations had organized their annual demonstration in support of the Cuban Revolution. Near the Zócalo the student demonstrators clashed with the police, and in the ensuing melee many protestors were injured and some killed. That same day the authorities sacked the central offices of the Communist Party.

By the end of July students from both the UNAM and the IPN had organized to go out on strike over six demands, including compensation for injured students, release of detained students and other political prisoners, disbanding of the riot police, and repeal of Article 145 of the penal code, which defines "crimes" of public disorder. Over the course of the next two months the students continued to strike and to engage in a variety of activities designed to win a wider base of public support and to force the government into negotiating with them on the six points of their petition. Massive protest marches, the take-over of public buses, graffiti, street theater, and extensive leafletting of the capital were the principal instruments of student propaganda. Beyond their specific demands, in the eyes of many the student movement also embodied broad hopes for a more open, democratic society, greater rights for workers, and a freer dialogue between those in power and those who, fifty years after the revolution, remained powerless. Faculty members of the two institutions created a committee in support of the reforms and in protest against the escalating police brutality and the incarceration of student activists.

Besides the UNAM and the IPN, several teachers' colleges, the Colegio de México, and the Universidad Iberoamericana joined the National Strike Committee (Comité Nacional de Huelga, CNH). The student movement's public protests attracted enormous numbers of people: 150,000 at the Zócalo on August 13, a march involving 300,000 on August 27, and tens of thousands at the famous "silent demonstration" of September 13. The government responded with increasingly repressive measures: police violence against protesters and onlookers, hundreds of arrests, attacks on school buildings occupied by the students, and finally, on September 18, the invasion and two-week occupation of the UNAM campus by the army.

Dramatic as these events were, for most people the definitive tragic confrontation between the movement and a government intolerant of opposition took place on October 2, 1968, when, at a peaceful rally at the Plaza de las Tres Culturas (Plaza of the

Three Cultures) in Nonoalco-Tlatelolco, army troops and police trapped thousands of demonstrators, indiscriminately fired on them, and pursued them into the surrounding apartment buildings. "La noche de Tlatelolco," the Tlatelolco massacre, left hundreds of demonstrators dead, thousands illegally detained, and many tortured in military camps. By the next morning the student movement was effectively destroyed and the city soon returned to a curious state of silence, calm, and disturbing "normality" as the opening day of the Olympics—October 12, "el día de la Raza"—drew near.[9]

In the aftermath of October 2, government cover-ups and censorship of the media impeded any investigation of the massacre and prevented effective dissemination of what scant information was available to the press.[10] The Olympics proceeded on schedule, and Elena Poniatowska has said with bitter irony that Mexicans applauded when an army lieutenant won a medal. But, in the years following 1968, Tlatelolco and the student movement have figured prominently in the intellectual, political, and artistic discourse of Mexico. A large and varied body of Tlatelolco literature has engaged in an analytical and critical confrontation with the events of 1968.[11] Such canonical writers as Octavio Paz, Carlos Fuentes, Rosario Castellanos, and Rodolfo Usigli wrote essays, poetry, and drama in response to the massacre and the overall political and economic climate.[12] Student activists, some writing from prison, found a voice by recording their own testimonies about their personal experience and the collective aspirations of the movement.[13]

The overwhelming majority of Tlatelolco literature vindicates the student movement and condemns Díaz Ordaz and his government for the violent suppression of the students' demands and activities, although a few texts make accusations of (communist) "outside agitation" behind the movement and defend the law and order measures taken by the authorities.[14] The political system, beginning in the Luis Echeverría presidency (1970–1976), also moved to accommodate—and neutralize—the forces for change by effecting a so-called democratic opening and instituting some electoral reforms. The inclusion of a broad range of opposition candidates for the first time in the 1982 presidential elections is perhaps the most dramatic manifestation of this opening. Opinions vary as to the lasting impact of 1968 on Mexican politics, but there can be no doubt that the Tlatelolco massacre, far from silencing the students' demands for dialogue, guaranteed an ongoing debate over the issues of repression, corruption, and monolithic exercise of authority which they raised.

LA NOCHE DE TLATELOLCO

Elena Poniatowska's *La noche de Tlatelolco*, a relatively early piece of Tlatelolco literature, remains the most widely read account of what Carlos Fuentes has called the "Mexican dilemma." [15] It has gone through forty-eight Spanish-language editions totaling almost a quarter of a million copies, and translations have been published in English, Polish, and Czech. An analysis of the process of production and the structure and language of the text reveals its semantic and aesthetic specificity as well as its connections to other works of testimonial literature. Two aspects of the book are of particular interest with regard to my study of dialogue in Elena Poniatowska's writing. They are the role of the nearly invisible editor of the text vis-à-vis the voices that she has recorded; and the intertextual relationship between the account of the events of 1968 and the series of sixteenth-century indigenous poems of the conquest of Mexico which appear halfway through *La noche de Tlatelolco*.

Elena Poniatowska's work recoups silenced voices and poses an effective challenge to official history in such a way that hierarchies of signification and authority are deconstructed and not merely reversed. While responding to an urgent need unambiguously to denounce the government suppression of the student movement, the text resists inscribing its history into a simple dichotomous scheme that would oppose guilty oppressors to innocent victims. Like many other *testimonios, La noche de Tlatelolco* contains its own self-critical gesture at the same time that it makes a strategic claim to a kind of truth about the events it portrays.

Elena Poniatowska has spoken many times about how, immediately after the October 2 massacre, she became involved in gathering the testimonies which would later form the basis of *La noche de Tlatelolco*. She recalls that on the night of October 2 three women came to her house to tell her about the terrible events they had just witnessed in Tlatelolco. Somewhat skeptical of what she had heard, Poniatowska went to Tlatelolco.

"I went on October 3 to see Tlatelolco. It shocked me to see the piles of empty shoes, to see the tanks there and the traces of machine gun fire all over the place. Then I said to myself, what happened here? (Because when the women came to tell me on the night of October 2 I thought they were hysterical.) I even saw blood on the wall, bloody handprints, and all the windows broken out. I saw that there had been a real battle there. After that I kept track of the testimonies of the people who told me their experiences, and that's how I put together the book."[16]

In the months that followed, driven to react to the government censorship of news relating to Tlatelolco, Elena Poniatowska sought out participants and witnesses to the activities of the student movement. She interviewed university and secondary students, parents, professors, workers, inhabitants of the Nonoalco-Tlatelolco housing complex, and other residents of the capital and foreign journalists such as the Italian Oriana Fallaci, who herself was injured at Tlatelolco. Poniatowska visited the military camps and prisons where thousands of people were detained, and she accumulated other materials pertaining to the student movement. This exhaustive effort of investigation signals Poniatowska's commitment to the students in the face of the repression they suffered. Poniatowska was also struck by the quick return to normality (silence and ignorance) in the capital, which she interpreted as a tacit complicity with the official violence.[17] Already a week after the massacre she felt "the outrage of knowing that such a thing had happened and yet everyone was so absorbed in watching the Olympics on the TV."[18]

The text that resulted from Elena Poniatowska's persistent research is a complex montage of many fragmented discourses. Poniatowska deconstructs the eyewitness accounts gleaned from her interviews by fragmenting them and then recomposing the distinct voices into a coherent but polysemic composition which no single speaker can dominate.[19] The fragments range from a few lines to half a page or a page in length, and interspersed among the testimonies are passages from a myriad of other sources: newspaper articles, speeches by government officials, protest songs and chants, graffiti, police records, and literary texts. Photographs are also introduced to complement the verbal representation. The montage form with its juxtaposition of heterogeneous elements creates a multilayered vision fraught with gaps, discrepancies, and contradictions, as well as startling moments of unanimity and consensus. By thus rejecting the homogenizing tendencies of much conventional journalism, a discourse which reduces and isolates events in a single synthetic capsule or "soundbite," Poniatowska has arrived at a highly effective form of presenting the silenced, marginalized other history of 1968.

Both structurally and thematically *La noche de Tlatelolco* confronts the tension inherent in the double, duplicitous nature of power: power as domination versus power as creative, enabling energy. The difficulty of engaging in the second practice of power without falling into the first is fundamental to the portrayal of the student movement in *La noche de Tlatelolco*. Starting with a reversal of the hierarchical relationship that places victor over vanquished, the book clearly privileges the voices of the defeated students over the discourse (characterized as a monologue) of the government. This inversion constitutes a necessary critique of the very real abuse of power that culminated in the Tlatelolco massacre. But such a reversal can simply reestablish a fixed hierarchy of values, threatening to reproduce the very monopoly of meaning against which the text is written. *La noche de Tlatelolco* escapes that trap by balancing out its condemnation of the Mexican government with the play of multiple and contradictory versions of how the student movement was configured and how it performed. For example, criticism of the movement's tactics and theoretical base, its leaders, its organization, and its limited contacts with workers and peasants comes from a variety of sources within and outside the movement. The many meanings, primarily positive but also negative, which the signifier "student movement" accumulates in the montage-text are a sign of the deconstructive capacity of this type of decentered, collective retelling of history. The fruition of the montage technique in turn demands an active reading which examines the editorial role of the "author" of the testimonies and unravels the intertextual dimensions of the book.

FRAMING QUESTIONS

The publication of *La noche de Tlatelolco* under the name of Elena Poniatowska raises issues of authorship which are somewhat different from those encountered in reading *Hasta no verte Jesús mío*. *La noche de Tlatelolco* is an oral history, a frequently cited and seemingly unambiguous example of Latin American testimonial literature. Many critics of *testimonio* refer to Miguel Barnet's 1970 essay, "La novela testimonio: Socioliteratura" (The testimonial novel: Social literature), and its concept of the self-effacing *gestor* (manager or director) as a point of departure for addressing the authorship of collaboratively produced texts. According to Barnet, the *gestor* must strip away his or her own individuality to assume that of the informant and of the collectivity which the informant represents. Barnet seeks out a representative protagonist, a "legitimate actor" in history, as his ideal narrator for the events that most affect the popular sensibility.[20] In writing *La noche de Tlatelolco* Elena Poniatowska first listened to hundreds of such witness-protagonists of 1968, and then she exploited her considerable authority as a journalist to foreground the discourse of the oppressed. By respecting the authority of her informants and by acting as a mediator between them and the reading public, Poniatowska, while not a member of the oppressed community, offers a positive model of the production of testimonial literature.

It is clear from the statement by Elena Poniatowska quoted earlier in this chapter that the victims of the violence themselves empowered the writer with the fundamental insight that led her to investigate the events of July to October 1968. The three women who came to Poniatowska's house on October 2 were followed in subsequent weeks by other witnesses anxious to tell their stories to the well-known journalist. Students, parents, and bystanders converted their personal outrage and fear into the energy to speak out against the violence they had suffered. Their initiative was matched by Poniatowska's active search for information on the student movement. Ironically, though, the writer's initial reaction of disbelief and the charge of hysteria confirmed the very same gender and political biases which the writing of *La noche de Tlatelolco* ultimately subverts. Therefore, the process of conducting the interviews and gathering the other materials which comprise the book can be seen as a constant give and take of discursive authority and responsibility among a variety of voices. On the one hand, the speaking subjects of the testimonies are collectively the "authors" of both the activities of the student movement and the language of its verbal recreation. On the other hand, a single compiler-writer, Elena Poniatowska, has transcribed, organized, and issued—"authored"—the history in written form.

In tribute to this double process Elena Poniatowska employs various strategies to efface her own individual presence and to emphasize the importance of the testimonial contributions. The apparent absence of a unifying, authoritative narrative voice and its replacement by an elusive editor who appears and disappears, who slips on and off the page, is a crucial narrative strategy in *La noche de Tlatelolco*. Other readers of the text have commented on this. In a book review of the English translation, Ronald Christ writes that "the narrator is no more visible here than a director who chooses what will be photographed or an editor who snips the *what* into the *how* we see." [21] Of course, this very snipping of the "what" into the "how" we see is itself a powerful wielding of narrative authority, suggesting as it does the deliberate manipulation of the many fragmented testimonies. [22] In spite of her intentions to give voice to others, Poniatowska cannot wholly abdicate her mediating authority, and the editorial figure is at once accessory and essential to the voices she records, marginal and central to their story.

This, then, is the basic framework upon which *La noche de Tlatelolco* rests: a reporter, not directly involved in the events portrayed, poses questions to many witnesses, records their testimonies, and frames the fragmented history into a verbal montage. The act of framing questions and an interrogation of the reporter/editor as a frame for the written work are inextricably linked issues in my reading of *La noche de Tlatelolco*. Working far afield from discussions of testimonial literature, Jacques Derrida identifies precisely the essential, intimate connection between frame and work which Poniatowska enacts in her writing of the oral history of the 1968 student movement. In his essay "The Parergon," which appeared in 1979 in the journal *October*, Derrida deconstructs a conventional opposition in the theory of aesthetics, the opposition of parergon to ergon, or frame to work, in order to show how a frame, far from being supplementary or extra to the work itself, is an integral part of it and plays an active role in its structure and meaning. Reexamining the definition of the term *parergon* as a "secondary or foreign object, accessory, frame, something exterior" to the work,[23] he demonstrates the complicit, interdependent relationship between the two apparently opposed concepts. Speaking primarily of visual art and architecture but with intriguing ramifications for our study of testimonial literature, Derrida affirms that the drapery cannot be ripped from the statue nor the colonnade from the palace, and so "it is not simply their exteriority which distinguishes them as *parerga*, but the internal structural link by which they are inseparable from a lack within the *ergon*."[24] The editor of *La noche de Tlatelolco* functions as this kind of framing figure, supplying a lack within the testimonies and inscribing herself into their story.

In the superficial configuration of *La noche de Tlatelolco* it is easy to distinguish the editor, as frame, from the "work itself." The editorial figure, identified by the initials "E.P.," is present only to collect and publish the essential voices, to let them speak and not to intervene in their narration. That is, she would, with Michel Foucault, "avoid the indignity of speaking for others."[25] That each testimony does indeed apparently speak for itself is graphically reinforced by the individual names which identify the fragments and by the blank space that separates each one from the next. But the self-sufficiency of the testimonies is only apparent, because the existence of the work as a published text does not stem solely from the independent energy of the testimonies. Contrary to appearances, it hinges as well on the authorizing labor of the frame, the editor, whose own considerable authority is revealed in the very gesture of empowering the other's speech. There is a necessary connection of work to frame, frame to work, which reminds us that the editorial function is neither neutral nor transparent but charged with meaning and with the making of meaning.

La noche de Tlatelolco begins with a series of photographs that capture images of the student movement: impressive views of mass marches, photos of the better-known student leaders, photos of students being arrested, being beaten, pictures of Tlatelolco moments before—and moments after—the shooting began, jail cells crowded with young people.[26] This visual frame anticipates and complements the testimonies, which are further delayed by a second frame, three introductory paragraphs signed by "E.P." and separated from the testimonies which constitute the "work itself." In this introduction the editor establishes an emotional atmosphere and inserts herself into the scene as a listening, observing "I." The atmosphere is euphoric, festive, self-confident: a scene of children off to a street fair, arm in arm. But, as the introduction makes clear, it will be a festival of death, a bloody carnival in which "the guns in the shooting gallery are aimed at them, children-targets, wonder-struck children, children for whom every day is a holiday until the owner of the shooting gallery tells them to form a line, like the row of tin-plated mechanical ducks that move past exactly at eye level, click, click, click, 'Ready, aim, fire!'" (*Massacre*, 3).[27] The frame, then, has given away the ending, which is revealed as the unexpected but inevitable explosion of violence. The frame, decisive from the start in preparing the readers' reception of the testimonies that follow, defuses the shock and also emphasizes the shocking nature of the material.

In addition to these paragraphs, four other passages within the text are signed "E.P.," including a newspaper article written by Poniatowska and an introduction to the second half of the book. The significance of her initials is double. On the one hand, it signals her presence and her responsibility for the content of a few, specific fragments. It makes the figure of the editor visible to the reader and establishes her authority. But on the other hand, by announcing that "here I am," "I wrote this," "this is my contribution," it implies that she is somehow absent from the great majority of the document, that she didn't intervene in a hundred other places. The initials "E.P." are, therefore, a strategy to erase the editorial presence and at the same time to make it very concrete by pretending to limit it to a few appearances. These appearances serve to make the editor's absence seemingly more natural. To quote again from Derrida, "That which produces and manipulates the frame sets everything in motion to efface its effect." [28]

The editor also manifests her presence in an occasional appearance as an interlocutor within some of the testimonies. In the form of "usted," "tú," or "Elena" the editor becomes a character within the other's narrative. Both of these examples of the direct intervention of the editor—as "E.P." and as interlocutor—create confusion between the work and the frame, between the interior and the exterior. They are ways in which the parergon explicitly defines itself in contrast to the ergon and at the same time as intrinsically inseparable from it. The editorial function, apparently secondary as narrative frame, begins to take on a central value in the meaning of the text.

Perhaps the most important interpretive function of the editor, the way in which she is most truly essential to the work, is not, however, carried out by her overt interventions. Rather, Elena Poniatowska's assumption of the conventional editorial tasks of the selection and ordering of diverse material turns *La noche de Tlatelolco* into a very carefully structured piece of writing. First, in numbers alone, the selection of voices heavily favors the student movement as opposed to the government point of view. Second, the spokespersons for the movement include student leaders, rank-and-file activists, professors, blue-collar workers, citizens who observed from the sidelines, parents, and schoolchildren. By portraying the student movement as representative of a broad spectrum of Mexican society, the editor has confirmed from the outset the democratic claims made by the students, and she has thus already invested the text with meaning, creating an image of democracy in action. In contrast to the lively dialogue carried out among the recorded voices of the movement, the official line is often conveyed by quoting written documents, legalistic language, or formally delivered speeches, all of which are monologic discourses that refuse dissent. Further, Poniatowska often omits the names of policemen, government officials, and prison guards, and their anonymity, in striking contrast to the careful notation of the students' names, dehumanizes the protagonists of the government's policies.

The final organization of the oral history derives from a thematic scheme which respects only secondarily the chronology of the events portrayed. The first half of the book, "Ganar la calle," rendered into English as "Taking to the Streets," covers the period from the beginnings of the movement in July 1968 through the experiences of the imprisoned students one or two years later. This part develops several important subthemes: the origins of the student movement, the anti-establishment attitude of the young people and the lack of communication between them and their elders, the rallies and marches, the demand for a public dialogue with the government, the torture of prisoners by police, the betrayal of the movement by a few individuals, and prison life. There are many references to the Tlatelolco massacre in "Taking to the Streets," but the story of October 2 is postponed until part 2, "The Night of Tlatelolco." The delay creates tension and a heightened sense of the inevitability of the massacre; furthermore, the second half of the book will be read with full knowledge of its multiple causes and consequences.

This overall arrangement of the testimonies crucially invokes the interpretive labor of the writer, who, while renouncing the privilege of direct commentary, nonetheless communicates a series of judgments regarding the authenticity of the testimonies. Within her thematic arrangement of the material she skillfully employs two additional structuring strategies to validate the vision of the defeated students. Repetition and juxtaposition are key devices by which the writer overcomes incredulity, combats the official li(n)e, and creates ironic moments which convey her interpretation of the many conflicting accounts. Repetition by many witnesses of the same story, even of the same details, is especially important within the context of a Mexican reading public which, in 1971, had relatively little and incomplete knowledge of the massacre. Censorship of news reports, dispersal of the bodies among many morgues and hospitals, the isolation of political prisoners from the general population, the lack of a complete, public investigation into the massacre, and the lapse in time between the events of 1968 and the publication of books which attempt to record and explain them account for the impact of Elena Poniatowska's work. *La noche de Tlatelolco* both fills in the gaps created by censorship and counters the distortions in the existing record.

The accounts of the October 2 massacre and of the officially sanctioned torture committed in the jails present the most disturbing picture to the Mexican public. In order to overcome any possible inclination in her readers to deny the veracity of the testimonies, Poniatowska incorporates a variety of documentary strategies which lend credence to the text. The photographs that appear at the beginning give powerful visual support to the testimonies that follow. Reiteration of coinciding versions of unspeakable acts of violence also overcomes any tendency toward disbelief. If one person, especially a politically marginalized person, speaks of electric shocks, of blows to the legs, feet, stomach, genitals, of weeks of incommunicado detention, of sleep and food deprivation, that report might be dismissed as an aberration or an exaggeration, an isolated case of the abuse of power. But the same story told by many individuals must be read as the institutionalization of violence and the systematic violation of human rights. In a text which renounces the investing of truth in a single, dominant voice, which indeed exposes the abuses perpetrated by monologic expressions of power, repetition is one way by which the dissident collective voice claims the authority of its experience and denounces the role of the established press as an instrument of the government.

Additionally, the deliberate and carefully chosen juxtaposition of material from different kinds of sources often creates, through a contrast of styles, an ironic effect that can heighten the semantic charge and the emotional impact of each individual fragment. In the following example a conversation between the author and her brother Jan leads into a short newspaper article about another student activist. The juxtaposition of two very different manners of reporting largely similar stories effectively communicates the editor-narrator's judgment about the terrible seriousness of the students' defiance of authority. This passage is also the only place where Poniatowska inserts her own experience in the form of a direct testimony, a witness on a par with the other voices of the student movement. Elena Poniatowska speaks first.

> "Why did you get home so late night before last?"
> "Because we were painting slogans."
> "Where?"
> "On the Palacio . . ."
> "On the Palacio de Hierro?" [a department store]
> "No, that wasn't where."
> "Well, what Palacio then?"
> "On the Palacio."
> "You mean the Palacio Nacional?" [the capitol]
> "Yeah."
> "Good heavens! You're stark raving mad! You might get killed! What's the matter with you? You're out of your minds!"
> "We're immortal . . . And besides, we planned the whole thing very carefully—the time, who was going to be the lookout, the getaway car with the motor running, how much paint we'd need— you forget, old girl, we're experts at painting slogans." (*Massacre*, 31)

The dialogue continues for half a page more, and then this newspaper article follows: "On November 17, 1968, a nineteen-year-old student—Luis González Sánchez—was killed by a police officer who had caught him painting Movement propaganda on a wall near the freeway" (*Massacre*, 32).

A sense of the fragile immortality of these naive experts is one effect of this juxtaposition. The dry, impersonal tone of the newspaper article starkly contrasts with Jan's enthusiastic claims to expertise; and González Sánchez's death betrays the students' sense of invulnerability. Dialogue is silenced by the monologue of power, whether expressed by the policeman's bullet or by the journalist's report. Jan's impetuous voice flickers out in the realization that a life has been lost, that the festival is indeed a bloody one. Early in the book, when the student movement is still being portrayed as a coalition of high-spirited youth, the editor inserts a warning of the grave consequences of their confrontation with the government.

Stepping outside the text itself, the high culture establishment of Mexico unwittingly offered Elena Poniatowska an additional opportunity to challenge both the political status quo and accepted notions of literary authorship and ownership when they awarded the prestigious Xavier Villarrutia literary prize to her for *La noche de Tlatelolco*. In an open letter to President Echeverría the "author" rejected the award, demanding to know who would give a prize to the dead students. In an interview with Lorraine Roses, Poniatowska recalls that "they told me that President Echeverría, who was President Díaz Ordaz's successor, would present the prize. . . . But President Echeverría was the Secretary of the Interior [in 1968]. Wouldn't he have known and been responsible for what the president did? . . . So I said I rejected the award . . . and that this wasn't a book written to be feted." [29] The content of her public statement as well as the gesture of disavowing one of the material benefits derived from her labor remind us of the highly political nature of *testimonio* and the writer's enhanced sense of responsibility to her subjects. The letter also demonstrates Elena Poniatowska's resistance to seeing herself co-opted by the very government that she criticizes. Luis Echeverría's regime made its own highly touted claim to political openness after the repressive rule of Díaz Ordaz, as if forgetting Echeverría's necessary complicity in his predecessor's policy as a cabinet member himself at the time of the 1968 student movement. Elena Poniatowska further believes that some intellectuals were too quick to buy into the new government's change of style.

The editor of *La noche de Tlatelolco* is, then, an eminently parergonal figure. She participates actively in the production of the work by "framing questions" of history, politics, and language, but she is careful to hide the evidence of her transforming labor. She exercises control over the material at the same time that she allows the individual voices to claim their own authority as witnesses and participants in the history told. Narrative authority is a power which the editor constantly wields and abdicates and which has no single origin or destination. The authority to speak and to be heard rests neither solely with the students nor with the writer-journalist but rather in the relationship among the testimonies and between these and the editor. Poniatowska, a nonparticipant in the 1968 student movement, in her role as "E.P.," the editor-parergon who positions herself outside the ergon, in recuperating a silenced past becomes an integral part of its present, the essential extra who guarantees its future.

If one now considers Elena Poniatowska's other published works, it becomes clear that the figure of the editor as I have described it is emblematic of her stance as a writer in her country. Once an outsider, a foreigner, through a constant and active searching out of the other she has created for herself a Mexican identity. Mexico has supplied a lack (of cultural roots, of history, of "home") that she felt in herself, and in her work Elena Poniatowska has recuperated for Mexico a part of itself, a part it may consider extra, secondary, or subordinate: the silenced voices, the anonymous faces, the darkened pages of history; society's margins, another kind of framing figure which in fact penetrates to the center of her nation's collective life.

OTHER HISTORIES

The "vision of the vanquished" so often represented by testimonial literature is written within and against the existing language of history, politics, and literature. *Testimonio* assumes the inherently distorted, partial nature of hegemonic discourse, which privileges the victors over the vanquished, and it presents its own truth as a corrective to the "official story." Renato Prada Oropeza is one among many readers to point out the necessary intertextuality of *testimonio*. "All testimonial discourse is referential and claims truth value; in addition, it is always intertextual because, explicitly or implicitly, it *assumes another* interpretation (another text) about its object (referent)."[30] Prada Oropeza is emphasizing here the relationship between *testimonio* and the dominant discourse to which it is opposed. I would add that a testimonial work may also interact with other *testimonios*, referring to them to strengthen its own vision and to express solidarity with other struggles. Further, testimonial literature participates in literary intertextuality in the broadest sense given to the term by contemporary theorists. *La noche de Tlatelolco* presents a fascinating and semantically rich case of intertextuality—an intertextuality that permeates its language and structure on all levels, effectively advancing its recuperative and denunciatory aims.

Intertextuality signifies the necessary and infinite relations between a given text and the semiotic practices—literary and non-literary—of the culture within which it is produced. Conscious or unconscious, named or anonymous, the intertextual relationship always implies a process of appropriation and transformation of existing discourses. Julia Kristeva, whose influential early work on intertextuality is based on the theory of the novel developed by Mikhail Bakhtin, traces the productivity of literary language to that very process. In her theoretical work *Le Texte du roman*, translated into Spanish as *El texto de la novela*, Kristeva refers to the novel—any novel—as a constant permutation of texts, an "intertextuality," because many words and lines taken from other texts cross the space of its pages.[31]

Kristeva's analysis meets the exigencies of both classic and modern *canonical* literature. In speaking of the dialogic or the polyphonic novel,[32] neither Bakhtin nor Kristeva considered testimonial literature, yet a work like *La noche de Tlatelolco* perfectly exemplifies a dialogic and critical stance toward the pre-existing discourses that create the conditions of its production and reception. In the encounter between two systems of signs (texts), one set of meanings is adopted and *adapted* into a new context, creating an open-ended process of signification. The dialogue enacted across the intertextual space thus reactivates existing signs, imbuing them with new significance, as Kristeva implies in a later essay where she speaks of a text as "an intersection of words (texts) where at least one other word (text) can be read. . . . any text is constructed as a mosaic of quotations; any text is an absorption and transformation of another."[33]

In *La noche de Tlatelolco* Elena Poniatowska has assembled a vast and intricate "mosaic of quotations." The direct incorporation of published newspaper articles, official documents, and literary texts constitutes only the most visible instance of intertextuality. Other intertextual operations employed by Poniatowska, as by all authors, include the transformation of conventional narrative modes and cultural signs. Finally, intertextuality is not only a condition of the writing of *La noche de Tlatelolco*, but it is also a strategy for active reading that reaches beyond Poniatowska's book to explore its many pre-texts. Among all the quoted materials, the book *Visión de los vencidos: Testimonios indígenas de la conquista* (1959; *The Broken Spears*, 1962) acquires unique status through the discovery of extensive and at times uncanny connections between its depiction of ancient events and the modern oral history. The productive intersection between the voices of the Mexican students of 1968 and the voices of indigenous witnesses to the sixteenth-century Spanish conquest of Mexico therefore significantly broadens both the semantic horizons of *La noche de Tlatelolco* and the historical implications of the experiences it relates. If we keep in mind that intertextuality does not signify a simple repetition of words or passages but rather a transformative and critical reworking of material in a new context, then our recognition of *Visión de los vencidos* can enrich and strengthen the critique that *La noche de Tlatelolco* undertakes.

Visión de los vencidos is a well-known anthology of Nahuatl texts translated into Spanish by Mexican scholar Angel María Garibay and edited by Miguel León-Portilla. The selections, taken from the principal indigenous sources extant today, describe the conquest of the Aztec empire by Hernán Cortés from the perspective of the vanquished people. The original manuscripts date from the sixteenth century, when, during and immediately after the period of conquest (1519–1521), Nahuatl scribes wrote down poems and histories of their encounter with the Spaniards. Bilingual Spanish priests also performed an important role by transcribing Nahuatl oral testimonies of indigenous informants into the Latin alphabet. Among the earliest such records produced by indigenous scribes are the poems of the *Manuscrito anónimo de Tlatelolco* (1528) and the chronicles of the manuscript *Unos anales históricos de la nación mexicana*, also dated 1528. Fray Bernardino de Sahagún collected a more complete series of accounts between 1548 and 1561 for his masterpiece *Historia general de las cosas de Nueva España*. These important chronicles have been preserved in the *Códice Florentino*. Also included in the *Códice Florentino* and the *Códice Aubin* (1567) is a pictographic record of many of the same events. In *Visión de los vencidos* León-Portilla has edited and ordered the many extant prose versions into a roughly chronological account of the conquest. A number of illustrations adapted from the two codices accompany the text, and the book ends with four poems of lament which reiterate the previous testimonies.

To begin to unravel the strands that connect two "visions of the vanquished" across four and a half centuries of Mexican history, we must go to the very center of *La noche de Tlatelolco*. There, in the anxious moments between "taking to the streets" and the Tlatelolco massacre, ancient voices decry the loss of an empire and sound a warning for the future. These voices speak through a poetic text adapted from the poems of *Visión de los vencidos* by incarcerated students of the 1968 movement. The students' ten-stanza reworking of the *cantares tristes* (songs of sorrow, or elegies), which Poniatowska has borrowed in turn, offers the primary and most visible point of contact between *La noche de Tlatelolco* and the indigenous chronicles. Placed at the structural axis of *La noche de Tlatelolco*, the poem has a double orientation back toward what has been read and ahead toward what remains to be told. For example, the capture of Cuauhtémoc reiterates the theme of the imprisonment and torture of student leaders already elaborated in "Taking to the Streets," while the images of blood, tears, and death anticipate the post-poned narrative of the massacre.

The poem "contained" in the pages of Poniatowska's book also encourages us to break through the limits of a linear reading by pulling our attention outside *La noche de Tlatelolco* toward its own "source" in *Visión de los vencidos*. If we accept the in-tertextual invitation and fully pursue the course it sets, we can recognize and interpret the presence of *Visión de los vencidos* in *La noche de Tlatelolco* not only in the quoted poems but also in other words and scenes disseminated throughout the modern text. For to discover that crucial, axial link is to see the stone thrown into the water and to follow its energy lapping out in waves to the very edges of the irremediably disturbed surface of the text.

My analysis of the dialogue between present and past fol-lows the forking paths and the switchbacks of a reading which moves back and forth between the two texts to discover an ever-expanding web of intertextual relationships. The quoted poems which set the process in motion were selected and edited by stu-dents in Lecumberri jail who thus acted as mediators between the two historical moments. Their modification of the Nahuatl poems to suit their own purposes and situation precedes Ponia-towska's editorial appropriation of the material, twice removed from its source.

The bibliographical information provided in *La noche de Tlatelolco* facilitates our finding four *icnocuícatl*, or elegies, in-cluded in the last chapter of *Visión de los vencidos*. Three of the four *icnocuícatl* appear in the modern adaptation: "Se ha per-dido el pueblo mexícatl," "Los últimos días de Tenochtitlán," and "La ruina de tenochcas y tlatelolcas" describe the defeat of the Mexicans and the flight from Tenochtitlán; the suffering of the people under siege by the Spaniards; and the final attack on the Aztec capital.[34] In a process similar to Elena Poniatowska's own deconstruction and reconstruction of the discourses of the student movement, the students themselves have fragmented, shuffled, and recomposed the seventy-one verses of the three *icnocuícatl* into a single forty-five-verse poem. Their reordering selects the following themes: violent death and the decay of dead bodies, the impossibility of self-defense, hunger and physical suffering, the capture of Cuauhtémoc, the cries of the besieged people, and the ultimate defeat of the nation. By omitting names and details specific to Aztec culture and the conquest, the ancient lament has been generalized to reflect more closely the events of 1968. This transformation, inevitable in any intertextual operation, signifies the students' appropriation of a privileged moment in the national history. In this way they affirm their own experiences by making an identification with their defeated but heroic ancestors. In the face of their political and legal disadvantage, the incarcerated students emphasize the common over the differential when establishing their claim on the past. Against an imposed silence, they forge a voice which is at once dissident and traditional in order to assert the authority—even the superiority—of the view from below.

A close analysis of one stanza from "Se ha perdido el pueblo mexícatl" shows how the intertextual effect extends far beyond the reading of the poem on pages 158–159 of *La noche de Tlatelolco*.

> Weep, my friends,
> you have heard the story, and you know now
> that we have lost our Mexican homeland.
> The water has turned bitter, our food has a bitter taste in our
>   mouths!
> This is what the Giver of Life has done in Tlatelolco.
> (*Massacre*, 167)

In their new context, these verses summarize and judge the disastrous effects of battle described in the preceding stanzas. The appellative mode includes us in the lament and evokes our compassion before the ancient and the modern tragedy. The verses also presage experiences recounted in the second half of *La noche de Tlatelolco* and recall testimonies from "Taking to the Streets." For example, scarcity of food and water caused enormous suffering among the Aztec people in 1521, and on the night of October 2, 1968, trapped inside their apartments by the presence of hostile troops outside, Poniatowska's informants testify to a cut-off of water, a lack of food, and the general terror of a state of siege.

Consider as well the ironic implications of the following intertextual references. The verse "This is what the Giver of Life has done in Tlatelolco" has at least two echoes in *La noche de Tlatelolco*. Early in the book a student says of President Díaz Ordaz: "We had to give voice to our indignation, hurl any and every insult we could think at this paternalistic figure, this *giver of life*, the great Tlatoani, our papa, God" (*Massacre*, 23, my emphasis). Díaz Ordaz, "Giver of Life," stands accused of presiding, like the Aztec gods, over a strictly hierarchical structure (political/religious), the Mexican pyramid with its place of blood sacrifice located at the apex. In their moment of greatest public support the students hurl insults at the diminished divinity of the president, who, nonetheless, godlike, refuses to appear before his human challengers. But by the time the whole verse is reproduced in the poetic text halfway through *La noche de Tlatelolco*, the "giver of life," whether secular president or divine authority, has clearly recovered his power to deal out death and destruction with impunity.

In a similar fashion to the examples chosen, virtually all the verses transcribed from the *icnocuícatl* have multiple echoes in the modern oral history. However, the intertextual dialogue between *La noche de Tlatelolco* and *Visión de los vencidos* is not limited to the transformation and dissemination of the poetic lament. A reading of both works in their entirety yields many more points of contact and an increasingly provocative "vision of the vanquished." It need not be assumed that all the parallel experiences, images, or structures that we may detect were intentionally set up by Elena Poniatowska, but rather as readers we construct and identify intertextuality through our own interpretive intervention in the work.

The structural resemblance between *Visión de los vencidos* and *La noche de Tlatelolco* is striking. Both books combine fragments from a variety of discourses, juxtaposing oral testimonies, written history, poetry, and visual media (painting or photographs) within a chronological trajectory. The collective and popular nature of the narrative voice is similarly evoked by the testimonial "we" of the Nahuatl speakers and the modern informants, equally members of a defeated, silenced group and equally opposed to a powerful plural other: Spanish conquistadores or Mexican government. However, in contrast to the anonymous and relatively homogeneous "we" of the indigenous community as recorded in *Visión de los vencidos*, the named witnesses to the events of 1968 constitute a notoriously divided group, a "we" which threatens to splinter into a proliferation of I's. But the solidarity also expressed by the victims of the repression counterbalances the centrifugal pull of internal divisions in the movement, as the students both validate and question their effectiveness in promulgating a program of social change. In another corresponding structure, behind the anonymous voices of *Visión de los vencidos* we recognize the mediating figure of Fray Bernardino de Sahagún, equivalent in a certain way to that of Elena Poniatowska. Both are interlocutors and chronicler/editors, carrying out the recuperation of a history that their own society seeks simultaneously to destroy.

The branching paths of an intertextual reading lead to a series of recognitions at the anecdotal level as well, common experiences which inexplicably connect the sixteenth and the twentieth centuries. The primary instance of intertextuality, the poetic text, stimulates an ever-broadening investigation of experiences and motifs from *Visión de los vencidos* that reappear in *La noche de Tlatelolco*.

The descriptions of arms and armed confrontation offer numerous links across time, beginning with the lopsided advantage held by the conquering forces. The Spanish with their horses and firearms and the present-day soldier equipped with tanks and machine guns enjoy an overwhelming military superiority. Stones become a sign of rage and impotence for the Aztecs as well as for the students, and one student points out precisely this connection when he says that "we fought the *granaderos* Aztec style: we threw stones" (*Massacre*, 73).[35] Right there in Tlatelolco, sixteenth-century warriors threw stones from the rooftops, as young people would also do on October 2, 1968.

Two specific military tactics employed by Cortés' men and

related in *Visión de los vencidos* eerily coincide with tactics of the Tlatelolco massacre. The use of disguises is one: "The Spanish soldiers often disguised themselves so that they would not be recognized. They wore cloaks like those of the Aztecs" (*Broken Spears*, 112). "Yesterday, October 2, I was put in command of two sections of cavalry troops . . . and given orders to take these two sections to the Tlatelolco housing unit, with my men and myself dressed in civilian clothes but wearing a white glove" (*Massacre*, 209). Another curious repetition, with disastrous consequences for both groups of aggressors, occurs when a military maneuver designed to trap civilians turns against the very soldiers involved in the action. The Spanish once built a huge catapult in the Tlatelolco market, but they miscalculated its design, and it threw the boulders against their fellow soldiers, to the amazement of their intended victims. "This seemed to cause an argument among the Spaniards: they gestured toward the Indians and shouted at each other" (*Broken Spears*, 111). On October 2, 1968, the disguised troops completely encircled the demonstrators, which resulted in stray bullets hitting other soldiers positioned across the plaza. "Many soldiers must have shot each other, because as they closed in on the Plaza, bullets were flying from all directions" (*Massacre*, 256). The authorities in 1968 manipulated the outcome of their own error by pointing to the injured soldiers as proof of an attack initiated by well-armed subversives. The torture of prisoners, the surprise attack on unarmed civilians, the closing off of escape routes and refusal to recognize surrender, and the theme of a festival which turns bloody are other parallel experiences that demonstrate a continuity of violent measures to impose or defend military-political control.[36]

Blood, rain, and tears stain the pages of both these histories of the vanquished and strengthen the impact of a combined, comparative reading. Rain connects three key moments in history: the Noche Triste of 1519, the final defeat of the Mexicans in 1521, and the Tlatelolco massacre of 1968.[37] In *La noche de Tlatelolco* the drops of rain mix with the tears of those who call for help or mourn their dead. "Everything was a blur—I don't know if it was because I was crying or because it had started to rain. I watched the massacre through this curtain of rain" (*Massacre*, 227). The rain that fell on the bodies of Spaniards and Aztecs, and centuries later on all those caught unaware in Tlatelolco, and the tears of their survivors are waters which may wash away the blood but which cannot wholly cleanse the stain of violence.[38] The cries of the people, their tears, made voice and voice made text/imony resist the erasure of forgetfulness, leaving indelible marks on the national history. "And all these misfortunes befell us. We saw them and wondered at them; we suffered this unhappy fate" (*Broken Spears*, 137). "In these pages there echo the cries of those who died and the cries of those who lived on after them" (*Massacre*, 199).

Finally, "la noche de Tlatelolco," dispersed, unstable sign, "ambivalent word"—event, text, site of encounter, temporal and spatial coincidence in histories of struggle and defeat—offers itself as the maximum realization of the dizzying intertextual spiral. An indigenous testimony recalls the killing of Mexicans by Spaniards in the Tlatelolco market in 1521: "On one occasion, four Spanish cavalrymen entered the market place. They rode in a great circle, stabbing and killing many of our warriors and trampling everything under their horses' hooves. *This was the first time the Spaniards had entered the market place*" (*Broken Spears*, 109, my emphasis). But, curiously, it was *not* the first time, nor would it be the last, that violence came to Tlatelolco. In *Tlatelolco, tres instantáneas* Carlos Martínez reveals an earlier, pre-Hispanic incident of war where the Unidad Nonoalco-Tlatelolco now stands. Already in 1473 Aztec warriors had fought against Tlatelolcas in the same marketplace during their own war of conquest. The memory of the ancient killing field seems to persist in the popular imagination. A twentieth-century woman resident of Nonoalco-Tlatelolco explains it this way: "I hear tell that our ancestors, centuries ago, slaughtered lots of people, right there in Tlatelolco: there was lots of bloodshed, and that's why there's a curse on the place. . . . It was the Aztecs who made those human sacrifices, I'm told, but I have no idea whether it's true or not. . . . For many years nobody wanted to live there" (*Massacre*, 125). Ambiguous and hazy though the knowledge is, it suggests links between the past and the present via a mediating space,

Tlatelolco, and a recurring violence. The danger hidden in the walls "red with blood," according to the ancient poet, breaks out to stain them again with blood. "There was also blood all over the walls; it seems to me that the walls of Tlatelolco are drenched with blood" (*Massacre*, 209).

It would be easy (but, I believe, false) to draw a pessimistic conclusion from the correspondences that I have traced. Any conclusion that affirms a fatal, inevitable cycle of violence in Mexican history runs counter to the text that we are studying and to Elena Poniatowska's thought. Consider how the writer responded to a question about Octavio Paz's praise for *La noche de Tlatelolco*: "I admire Octavio Paz very much . . . but I don't agree with one of his theses about Mexican history. He maintains that the Plaza of the Three Cultures is a place of sacrifices, and that because we have Aztec ancestors we are condemned cyclically to slaughter a great number of people. This thesis is highly debatable . . . It's not possible to say that because we carry within us the *potential* for human sacrifice, we retain across the years the *need* to kill." [39] To resist reading a cyclical image of history into these texts, it is important to underscore again the transformational dimension of intertextual relationships. The coincidences may fascinate us, but significant differences also separate the two discourses of the vanquished which we have studied. *Visión de los vencidos* and *La noche de Tlatelolco* expose and criticize the potential for violence that exists in material conditions which are historically determined and intelligible to the discerning reader.

Aztec science and religion, fatalistic and mythocentric, may well have predicted the empire's defeat at the hands of mysterious strangers from across the sea. And when indigenous poets lament that "we have lost the Mexican nation" they are commemorating a rupture with the past so radical as not to permit a projection toward the future. But in 1968, in the other, future Mexico born in that moment of loss four hundred and fifty years before, in today's *mestizo* Mexico, its citizens must understand differently the meaning of violent confrontation and defeat. When a student says that "Tlatelolco is the dividing point between these two Mexicos" (*Massacre*, 6), he affirms that Tlatelolco is not only a place of sacrifice but also a site of revelation and unmasking that can lead to an effective critique of the monologue of monopoly power and institutionalized violence. The vision of the conquered, recuperated in Elena Poniatowska's text, participates in this critique, breaking the silence which is complicit with repression. By carrying out a dialogue with the silenced protagonists of 1968 and with the Mexican past, *La noche de Tlatelolco* and Elena Poniatowska oppose the monolithic discourse of authority and propose a creative, responsible distribution of discursive power.

FOUR

INTIMATE CONVERSATIONS
Fictions of Privilege

T he prominence accorded to *Hasta no verte Jesús mío, La noche de Tlatelolco, Fuerte es el silencio,* and *Nada, nadie* among Elena Poniatowska's published titles has determined the popular perception of her as a writer who is primarily committed to listening to other voices and narrating other lives to the virtual erasure of her own likeness from the page. Well-worn phrases such as "champion of the oppressed" and "voice of the powerless" attest to the strength of her reputation as a self-effacing medium for the silenced, suppressed histories that lie beyond the official story. Poniatowska herself speaks of being a vehicle at the service of others, and her advocacy is founded upon her constant engagement in dialogues across class, ethnic, linguistic, political, and gender lines.[1]

Correspondingly, Elena Poniatowska has often professed a deep-rooted reluctance to speak or write directly about herself, and in interviews she characteristically turns the topic of conversation away from her own work and life. In response to our questions, Poniatowska is likely to evoke the names of certain indispensable psychic companions (Rosario Castellanos, Carlos Monsiváis, Jesusa Palancares, Josefina Bórquez, Simone Weil), recharging their words with new energy and deflecting our attention away from the subject at hand. A measure of guilt and class responsibility and the sense that her own experiences are never as interesting as someone else's inhibit direct self-revelation by the author.

However, self-discovery may take numerous direct and indirect forms, as we have seen in the analyses of *Palabras cruzadas*, *Hasta no verte Jesús mío*, and *La noche de Tlatelolco*. There dialogue involves equally an encounter with the other and an exploration and extension of the self, even when it is overtly focused on the other's story. In her interviews with the diverse and disparate characters exemplified by Alfonso Reyes, Josefina Bórquez, and the students of 1968, Poniatowska has achieved a sense of personal belonging which both assimilates and challenges the competing ideologies of Mexican society. In addition, I have shown that the mediation of another's words always implies an act of transformation in which the mediating authority—no matter how disguised—plays an essential role. As a result, the works studied thus far pay tribute to the interdependence between public conversation and private concerns, and between projection toward the other and construction of the self. Specifically for Elena Poniatowska, this means that her engagement with the other does not supersede but rather is closely linked to her interrogation of the multiple and conflicting subject positions that she herself occupies.

In this chapter I resist the author's deflecting gestures to concentrate on a group of more obviously self-reflective texts. For in spite of her disclaimers, Elena Poniatowska has indeed frequently recorded more "intimate conversations" in her written work. *Lilus Kikus*, first published in 1954, the short stories collected in *De noche vienes* (1978), the 1988 novel *La "Flor de Lis,"* and the autobiographical essay "A Question Mark Engraved on My Eyelids" (1991) counter the writer's notorious reticence to talk about her own experience and about members of her family and her social class by presenting a sustained scrutiny of worlds close to home. And although it could be argued that as a writer Elena Poniatowska is "at home" virtually anywhere in Mexican society, I am speaking here of home as that world into which she was born and to which she always returns: the world of economic and social privilege in the midst of poverty, and the world of women within patriarchy.

Although they were written simultaneously with the interviews, testimonies, and chronicles that are, for many readers, the hallmark of Poniatowska's career, these texts stand apart from other titles because they were not undertaken on assignment nor out of a sense of duty but for the author's own pleasure. Elena Poniatowska has said that "activism is a constant element in my life, even though afterwards I anguish over not having written 'my own things.'"[2] She completes many of her books as *mandas*, promises or vows which must be kept, tasks which fell to her, often not of her own choosing. But the short fiction and La *"Flor de Lis"* answer willingly to that personal anguish, and they overcome the tendency toward silence and self-censorship.

Bell Gale Chevigny has rightly identified Elena Poniatowska's life-long preoccupation with the "equivocal privilege" of class position and with the gilded cage of feminine dependency.[3] In *Lilus Kikus, De noche vienes,* and La *"Flor de Lis"* Poniatowska creates a fascinating cast of upper-class and middle-class female protagonists from young girls to mature women, and she incorporates a wealth of autobiographical detail to carry out a critique of the alienating effects on the individual and on social relations of class hierarchy, racism, Eurocentrism, cultural imperialism, and the consumer society.[4] The author uses her own intimate knowledge as the daughter of an aristocratic family, born an authentic Old World princess, to ask what is at stake in maintaining and in challenging the investment in privilege and sheltered subordination. Thus the stories are fictions about the privileges attendant upon wealth and skin color, and they are texts which show privilege to be a fiction, and a harmful fiction—a product of human language and human structures of power and a lie based on the illusion of inherent and inherited superiority. These titles elaborate a more personal perspective on Elena Poniatowska's continuing challenge to patriarchal values (both social and literary) and her deconstruction of the prerogative of class. The short stories and La *"Flor de Lis"* also raise different questions of narrative voice, language, verisimilitude, and authorial responsibility from those posed by the documentary texts.

Lilus Kikus was Elena Poniatowska's first published book, appearing in 1954 to initiate the series "Los Presentes" edited by Juan José Arreola. The twelve connected narratives of *Lilus Kikus* are a "schematic *Bildungsroman*" which depicts a young girl confronting increasing limits to her behavior and her aspirations as she moves from childhood into adolescence.[5] Lilus leads a somewhat solitary life, finding amusement in improvised toys and games which she creates using found objects and her fertile imagination. She prefers to be outdoors, she loves to ask questions, and she is a keen observer of the words and actions of others. An inveterate daydreamer, Lilus rebels against the order of the adult world and the adult imperative to be constantly "doing something." The world of the child and the world of the adult are clearly defined as opposing realms of freedom and confinement, spontaneity and discipline, curiosity and "book-learning." The author works with conventional narrative materials, including an all-seeing external narrator, straightforward passages of description and dialogue, and an emphasis on everyday activities to portray the events of childhood in an understated manner. But the simple language and the ingenuous tone belie Poniatowska's sophisticated insights into the girl-child's problematical accession into adulthood. Repeated images of disappointment, anguish, and loss represent maturity as a blunting of the child's potential, and Lilus' sharp eye detects the contradictions and the hypocrisy of her superiors. "La tapia," for example, begins and ends with a scolding, first given by a female servant and then by Lilus' mother. The motive for the reprimand is the protagonist's "excessive" curiosity and activity, and the lesson is imparted by women who have long since grown up in obedience to patriarchal strictures.

Adolescence, viewed as a period of transition and transformation, a period fraught with particular dangers for the female child, continues to fascinate Elena Poniatowska in her later stories and in the novel La "*Flor de Lis*." The ambivalence that Lilus Kikus feels toward her future and her precarious pose on the edge of definitive changes are evoked metaphorically by the image of her walking on the beach, one foot in the ocean and one on the sand; or in the city, one shoe on the sidewalk and the other off to the side "siempre algo desnivelada" (always a little off-balance).[6] The Lilus Kikus pieces were reissued in 1967 along with twelve short stories under the title *Los cuentos de Lilus Kikus*. With the exception of Bruce-Novoa's article, which I have cited, they have received little critical attention, a neglect due in part to their having gone out of print and to the tremendous success of later books which have overshadowed these early fictions.[7]

De noche vienes repeats some of the twelve new stories of the 1967 *Cuentos* and adds eight previously unpublished narratives. The volume features urban female protagonists from across the social spectrum. Several are young women caught in love relationships characterized by a lack of communication, rejection, inertia, and loneliness.[8] Other stories treat problems of exploitation and dependence in the mistress-servant relationship, the decadence of aristocratic values and ways of life, and the durability of social class divisions.[9] In some of the stories, ill-conceived attempts at rebellion end in defeat for the protagonist, showing that it is futile, even dangerous, to plot change on the deceptive coordinates of guilt and ignorance. Without offering a positive alternative to deeply ingrained patterns of behavior, the stories of *De noche vienes* do effectively expose some of the consequences of female subordination and class conflict in Mexican society.

In her fiction Elena Poniatowska skillfully employs humor and irony as instruments of her critique, as in "Cine Prado," "Esperanza número equivocado" (Esperanza wrong number), and the title story, "De noche vienes" (The night visitor). This wonderful parody of the sexual double standard and the "Institutional Revolutionary" bureaucracy features Esmeralda, a nurse who manages a career and five simultaneous marriages, all the while dutifully caring for her ailing father. At her trial for bigamy "in the fifth degree" the male judge expresses his exasperation at the defendant's lack of guile and utter candor, while outside the courthouse a group of women organize a demonstration in her support. Both the judge's charges of immorality and the display of feminist solidarity are equally incomprehensible to the innocently subversive Esmeralda. Sentenced to a jail term, Esmeralda receives frequent visits from her five husbands, numerous officials of the court, and even the judge, all of whom now regret their role in her prosecution. A number of published articles provide a groundwork of analysis on *De noche vienes.* Mónica Flori explores the questions of social stratification and woman's internalization of her oppression in two articles that study "El limbo" (Limbo), "La casita de Sololoi" (Sololoi house), and "Métase mi prieta entre el durmiente y el silbatazo" (Slide in my dark one, between the crosstie and the whistle).[10] Cynthia Steele's 1989 essay, "The Other Within," proposes that the mistress-servant relationship can function positively as a form of female complicity against patriarchy across barriers of class and race. Poniatowska picks up the threads spun by the stories of *De noche vienes* in the more complex verbal tapestry of *La "Flor de Lis,"* the focus of this chapter.

As many as fifteen or twenty years ago, Elena Poniatowska explained her preference for writing about oppressed, marginalized people and not her own social group with remarks that shed light on the apparently long incubation period of her 1988 novel. "I've always been afraid of creating something of my own, of writing. I have been able to write short stories, but not a novel out of my imagination only."[11] When pressed about her reluctance to create upper-class characters she replied, "In part I did it to avoid who I am. Someday when I have achieved a certain serenity, I will be able to create novels that aren't assigned tasks . . . write another novel about my family."[12] By the early 1980s she began to announce her intentions to write about her own world, "la reacción," as soon as other projects were complete. As it turned out, the writing of *La "Flor de Lis"* did not wait for a convenient break in the author's schedule. Rather, its composition both preceded by many years and coincided with the work on one such urgent self-assigned task, the earthquake chronicles of *Nada, nadie.* The story of when and how Poniatowska wrote *La "Flor de Lis"* has its own intrigue, and it pertains directly to the way that I have organized my analysis of the novel.

In the fall of 1985, while engaged with other members of her literature workshop in the exhausting labor of gathering and editing the earthquake testimonies, Elena Poniatowska began to write what would become the first 110 pages of *La "Flor de Lis."*

She embarked on the story of a young girl and her relationship with her mother as a kind of diversion from each day's painful encounters with destruction and tragedy in Mexico City. She continued to write throughout 1986 and into 1987, but multiple demands on her time and the pressure of an upcoming teaching stint at the University of California at Davis (fall quarter 1987) prevented her from completing the novel as she had begun it. In an effort to wrap up the book for submission before her departure for the United States, Poniatowska retrieved a manuscript, "El retiro" (The retreat), that she had written while on a government grant in 1957. The never-published "El retiro" narrates a Lenten religious retreat for young women and introduces the character of a half-mad, half-visionary French priest, Jacques Teufel. This thirty-year-old piece became the nucleus for the second half of La "Flor de Lis." Poniatowska now expresses regret over patching together the novel that she had begun as a way to conserve moments of pleasure in the midst of suffering. "The first part of La 'Flor de Lis' is probably the easiest writing I have done in my life. It's too bad that I didn't carry it through to the end in that same tone, and that I added on the part about the priest." [13]

Indeed, the two parts are not entirely successfully integrated, and I remember feeling puzzled in my initial reading at the sudden change in tone, language, and cast of characters that occurs on page 114. Undaunted, I was able to justify that the episode does fit into the novel's chronological scheme, and I discerned a certain logic in the protagonist's shift from the mother to the priestly father-figure as object of her love. The realization that editorial exigencies and not aesthetic or ideological requirements primarily determined the structure of the text somewhat tempered my analytical flights of fancy without nullifying the effect that the novel's composition has on the reader. La "Flor de Lis" merits the thorough reworking that Poniatowska would like to give it, but once again the economics of publishing constrain the writer's desires. The editors at Era find it more feasible simply to reissue the 1988 edition rather than to accommodate an extensive rewriting. Poniatowska does intend to revise the novel, probably cutting back on the Teufel/retreat chapters, when plans for an English translation are finalized.

La *"Flor de Lis,"* a novel of a young girl's development, follows the life of its single protagonist through her formative years (age seven to seventeen or eighteen) and portrays her quest for self-knowledge and identity. As such it participates in the Western tradition of the *Bildungsroman*.[14] Mariana, the novel's narrator-protagonist, is the daughter of a wealthy family of French, North American, and Mexican background. She was born in France but moved to Mexico with her mother, Luz, and her sister, Sofía, during World War II. There the Mexican maternal grandmother welcomes them into her home and into a new life which, nevertheless, continues to be dominated by European cultural values and the French language. The bulk of the novel is set in 1940s Mexico City, where Mariana leads the life of a typical "niña po-poff": private school, music lessons, parties, party dresses, trips to the countryside, Catholicism, two years at a convent school in the United States, friendships and phone gossip, and enduring but ambivalent relationships with her family's domestic servants. The enclosed spaces of home, patio, chapel, private automobile, and convent set the limits to feminine activity and, for the most part, to feminine interests and curiosity.

On the anecdotal level, the episodes involving Father Jacques Teufel offer the most excitement and disruption, introducing elements of intrigue, proscribed sexuality, and social protest. Otherwise the novel emphasizes the daily routine in order to explore the dynamics of Mariana's family relationships, her understanding of sex roles and social position, her formal education, and her particular sense of uprootedness as a French native actively discouraged from identifying with her Mexican roots. At the end of the novel the French priest has been forced to leave the parish, Mariana's sister is preparing to marry, and Mariana herself, facing a possible trip to Europe, begins to question the meaning and worth of her aristocratic heritage. The final pages leave open Mariana's future: perhaps rebellion and perhaps conformity with her family's expectations.

The subject matter of La *"Flor de Lis"* and the peculiarities of how it was written invite a joint, dialogical analysis of the novel and the short fictions of *Lilus Kikus* and *De noche vienes*. If La *"Flor de Lis"* is a *parche* (mending patch), or better yet a patchwork of pieces fortuitously stitched together across a three-decade span, then it seems appropriate to work related intervening material into its open-ended and imperfect design. As "fictions of privilege" all founded upon autobiographical elements and written in overlapping fashion during a thirty-year period, certain of Poniatowska's stories and the novel intersect and interact in a complementary fashion. I place La "Flor de Lis" at the center of my reading, because it is the longest piece and it presents the most complete development of characters, circumstances, narrative perspective, and imagery. But in the analysis of La "Flor de Lis" I also draw on selected short stories which elaborate connected motifs and experiences and which pursue other perspectives not accommodated in the chronologically narrated, autodiegetic novel. "El convento" from the original Lilus Kikus and "El limbo," "El inventario," and "De Gaulle en Minería" from De noche vienes form the nucleus of texts most closely implicated in Elena Poniatowska's intimate conversations.[15]

The close resemblance of these fictions to other nonfictional versions of Elena Poniatowska's "own life" (essays, interviews) should not blind us to the fact that autobiography and the autobiographical are loaded terms in today's theoretical vocabulary. As such we must use the autobiographical label with care, and, for historical reasons, with particular care in regard to writing by a woman. The explosion of research on the genre of autobiography since the late 1960s participates in the contemporary debate over the ideas of authenticity, referentiality, identity, and truth value in literature and, indeed, in all written discourse. Coexisting theories of autobiographical acts, pacts, and readings, despite their differences, coincide in rejecting any simple identity between person and story, existence and text, even in the most deliberately conceived work of self-representation.[16]

Beyond these concerns, women writers have encountered a gender-specific dilemma with regard to autobiography. Domna Stanton points out in The Female Autograph that all female writing has been historically decoded and denigrated as autobiographical, in the sense of narrowly personal, non-transcendent, and narcissistic.[17] This traditional devaluation logically leads some women writers to protest against characterization of their writing as primarily autobiographical. Elena Poniatowska has testified to her own vacillation before readings that stress the autobiographical in her work. On the one hand, *Lilus Kikus* is "a story of childhood, a story that may be autobiographical, or perhaps woven of the lives of several friends of the same age and with similar experiences. . . . The part about the convent was also a chapter from my own experience."[18] "The book [*Flor*] does have autobiographical elements. . . . I think all literature is autobiographical."[19] On the other hand, Poniatowska bristles at the suggestion that her fiction is limited to a recounting of her life story. "I don't know why this happens to me, but everything I write they identify with me. I think one has a right to fiction and imagination, no?"[20]

It is not my purpose to study the selected texts as autobiographical writing per se nor to posit identity where I discern resemblance. But it would be absurd to ignore the easily drawn correspondences between these and other versions of the "facts" of Elena Poniatowska's life. Throughout my book the concepts of positionality and of a subject-in-process and the idea of memory as already an interpretation (as is experience itself) have been integral to the reading of Elena Poniatowska's writing. Those concepts continue to function in my study of the specific ways in which, in *Lilus Kikus, De noche vienes*, and *La "Flor de Lis,"* Elena Poniatowska is on speaking terms with her individual past and with the ideological formations of her culture.

CLOSE-UPS OF THWARTED DEVELOPMENT

Feminist inquiries into the *Bildungsroman* have opened up the category to include representations of individual development that differ significantly from the classic narratives of European male self-realization and socialization which established the genre in the eighteenth century. The editors of *The Voyage In: Fictions of Female Development*, for example, bring together essays that focus on gender-based features of fictions of development and on the differences that gender makes in literary production. Diverse though the essays are, they find a common ground in the concept of development itself and in the importance of a time span and a social context within which development occurs.[21] La "Flor de Lis" clearly fits into this more flexible notion of the Bildungsroman, and it shows striking affinities to other examples of the genre written by twentieth-century women, including the stories of Clarice Lispector's Family Ties. Therefore, although my analysis is not comparative, I employ the term Bildungsroman mindful of its history and of the associations it may create in the reader's mind. I have three questions to ask of La "Flor de Lis" and, secondarily, of Lilus Kikus and De noche vienes: What image of female development is conveyed in the novel and how is it constructed? What is the significance of the relationship between Mariana and her mother, Luz? How do these literary representations of female development perform a critique of ethnic and social class privilege as understood by the female "beneficiaries" of that privilege?

La "Flor de Lis" begins in France when Mariana is seven years old, and it ends in Mexico City approximately ten years later. The chronological scheme and the experience of repeated geographical dislocations seem to duplicate the traditional male pattern of a linear, progressive Bildung of the protagonist toward independence through encountering a variety of choices and conflicts. But conversely, throughout her narration, Mariana's obsessive return to the figure of her mother works to undermine the notion of her development as a trajectory toward a desired and desirable autonomy. Luz is the emotional and structural axis of the novel, but she is an elusive, moving center around whom the narrator's words revolve in an unending spiral of love and longing. As a result, Mariana represents neither the achievement of the separation and singularity privileged by male-dominated models of development nor the success of strong attachments and relationships which some theories attribute to female psychological growth.[22] Seen in its totality, La "Flor de Lis" presents an image of female development thwarted by a combination of social and familial factors. Mariana's docility, her persistent fear of not belonging, and her constant need for approval and validation in the eyes of others are the signs of failed relationships. Particularly acute is the reader's sense, not necessarily shared by Mariana, that her attachment to the absent mother is an investment in loss and emptiness. "Todo con tal de que me quieran" (17–18): this single, poignant phrase—"Anything, just so they love me"—captures the anxious, self-defeating dependency that characterizes much of Mariana's behavior and her ambivalent assessment of her own self-worth. Around the motif of unrequited love, La "Flor de Lis" constructs its key elements of narrative perspective, visual imagery, and diverse linguistic and cultural registers in a ground-breaking portrayal of female childhood and adolescence in Mexican literature.

Lilus Kikus and many of the stories of De noche vienes employ an omniscient narrator external to the story; however, beginning with the creation of Jesusa Palancares, Elena Poniatowska has increasingly shown a preference for first-person narrator-protagonists. The choice of Mariana to be the principal narrator, focalizor, and character of "her" novel has important structural and thematic consequences for the text, as it did for Hasta no verte Jesús mío.[23] But the similar narrative technique plays out quite differently when applied to new and dissimilar materials. In stark contrast to the panoramic, self-critical vision of Jesusa Palancares, Mariana's self-narration conveys the more limited experiences, sites of action, and judgments of a sheltered young girl just beginning to see beyond the circle of home and family. Where temporal and emotional distance characterizes the highly charged relationship between the narrating and narrated I's of Jesusa Palancares, qualities of proximity and intimacy color Mariana's self-portrait. When compared to the portrayal of Jesusa, the radically different time frame in La "Flor de Lis" and Mariana's very different upper-class status and her youthfulness define unique possibilities and constraints for her vision of self and other. The first paragraph of the text provides a condensed glimpse of the novel's structure and its thematic preoccupations.

La veo salir de un ropero antiguo: tiene un camisón largo, blanco y sobre la cabeza uno de esos gorros de dormir que aparecen en las ilustraciones de la Biblioteca Rosa de la condesa de Ségur. Al cerrar el batiente, mi madre lo azota contra sí misma y se pellizca la nariz. Ese miedo a la puerta no me abandonará nunca. El batiente estará siempre machucando algo, separando, dejándome fuera. (13)[24]

A speaking I provides an eyewitness view of an event and of a disappearing other. A child, soon to be identified as a daughter, Mariana, gives testimony to her experience of separation and exclusion from her mother, reliving a feeling of abandonment that will not abandon her, ever. "Ese miedo a la puerta no me abandonará nunca." Doors often slam shut before Mariana's eyes, but the present-tense narration reopens the scene and re-creates the immediacy of the childhood episode, while the future time of "abandonará" points to a narrating consciousness located in an older Mariana. Unlike Jesusa in *Hasta no verte Jesús mío*, however, the older, narrating Mariana remains nearly invisible in *La "Flor de Lis,"* giving the impression that the child's experience is reenacted directly before our eyes. The use of the present tense, although not sustained with complete consistency, is a striking feature of the book, and it communicates the idea that the young Mariana is still very much alive in the implied future adult. True to the child's perspective, the mother appears in the guise of a character out of children's literature. The association suggests as well a childish or childlike quality in the mother which is further reinforced by the gesture of slamming the door. Indeed, Mariana does live out her youth surrounded by childish, self-absorbed adults: her mother infantilized by her conformity to the double bind of feminine dependency and upper-class frivolity; and her father incapable of love for reasons that his young daughter can only partially understand.

I have already described the chronological scheme of the story and its division into two major parts: the protagonist's young girlhood, which focuses on the mother as love object; and her crucial adolescent encounter with the priest, Jacques Teufel, to whom Mariana temporarily turns in search of a father figure. Within the linear plan, the episodic nature of the narrative is significant for the depiction of thwarted development. Mariana narrates the story, particularly in the first part, as a series of loosely connected vignettes, and she makes little attempt to account closely for the passage of time. She leaves dates, corresponding ages, and duration of episodes imprecise, as if the years have had scant impact on her. Mariana seems not only to speak but also to live within a timeless present, ever immersed in the moment. Transitions are abrupt and relationships of cause and effect are weak, thus reflecting the child's inability to analyze her own experiences or to understand the conditions that determine them.

An examination of significant moments recorded in the novel shows how the constriction of narrative perspective to the child-Mariana and the apparent lack of distance between narrator and focalizor effectively communicate the protagonist's uncritical assimilation of familial expectations and cultural phenomena. Mariana's avowed willingness to do everything "con tal de que me quieran," in contrast to her rebellious sister Sofía, signals one of her outstanding character traits: obedience. Obedience to individual superiors (family members, teachers, religious figures) and obedience to the norms of behavior observed in her social group guide Mariana's actions, even when good reason exists to disregard decorum. Her unthinking observance of good manners, for example, has humorous consequences one day at lunch. "Ni mi hermana ni yo decimos pío. 'Children should be seen and not heard,' advierte mi abuela Beth. . . . Un mediodía mi mamá olvida cortarnos la carne, a Sofía y a mí" (13–14).[25] Not daring to speak up, the two "duquesitas" wait in silence as the others eat, and they watch as the manservant eventually removes their untouched plates, provoking their mother to laughter over her forgetfulness. In another scene a new governess draws an uncomfortably hot bath, but Mariana climbs in, hoping that Mademoiselle won't notice anything amiss. Good manners also discourage the expression of emotions, the asking of questions, and the making of demands. Although the concrete situations—a meal, a bath, a walk in the park—are often ordinary and even amusing in their triviality, the overarching lesson that proper behavior dictates obedience, silence, and docility has crippling consequences for the growing child.

On a more serious plane, Mariana's parents and their friends, all with roots in the landed classes, manifest social class and ethnic prejudices that protect their sense of superiority against the demands of a changing society. For the most part Mariana internalizes their attitudes and shares their pride of inherited status and inherited objects. In school in Mexico City she once makes friends with the daughter of a bourgeois Jewish family. When Thérèse Nissan, a serious artistic student, invites Mariana to dinner at her home, the whole experience is a revelation. The Nissan family lives in an uncomplicated comfort that contrasts wildly with the elaborate splendor of Mariana's grandmother's European-style home. The Nissans' house is furnished with Mexican things bought at the local market, and their bedrooms are set up as art studios: plain and filled with light. At the table Thérèse and her family serve themselves from common platters and eat off earthenware dishes. Their manners challenge the exclusivity of Mariana's notions of well-bred behavior, because they are so strikingly different and yet not at all lacking in "good taste." Upon returning home, however, the protagonist is disturbed when her parents comment that her new friends are Jews, their enchanting customs are merely Jewish, and one day, they predict, Thérèse will cheat her because she is just a little Jew. The shift from narration to recreated dialogue at this moment puts the damning words into someone else's mouth, but Mariana is nonetheless influenced by her parents' scathing opinions. Gradually Mariana's confusion erodes her friendship with her sensitive classmate, and although she claims that she wants to live like Thérèse's family someday in the future, for now the Nissans disappear from view, diminished in Mariana's eyes by class and religious intolerance.

Education and the school as a site of socialization are principal themes of the traditional novel of development and of Elena Poniatowska's fictions of privilege. The final story of *Lilus Kikus*, "El convento," shows the main character preparing to go to a convent boarding school, and it relates her arrival at the school and her adjustment to the new routine. In "El convento" Lilus initially expresses numerous objections to her parents' decision to send her away to school, and she imagines with horror the loss of freedom that this change will entail. But her preconceived vision of the nuns as monstrous creatures devoid of human emotion melts before the favorable impression that the sweet, slender sisters immediately create. Soon Lilus not only tolerates but loves her school, the nuns, and the stories they intone in sad yet innocent voices. In *La "Flor de Lis"* Mariana and Sofía, too, set off to a Catholic boarding school—far away in the United States—soon after the birth of a long-awaited third child, a coveted son, Fabián. In its elaboration of the convent school experience, *La "Flor de Lis"* picks up on the earlier admiring depiction of the nuns and develops the theme of Mariana's successful integration into the strict regimen.

Under the nuns' tutelage, Mariana and Lilus Kikus receive similar lessons about Catholic dogma, the social hierarchy, and conventional sexual mores. Virginity until entering into marriage to a wealthy man, passivity within marriage, and a tolerant view of adultery are the recommended course for these daughters of privilege. But in both texts irony subverts the surface portrayal of the protagonists' acquiescence to expectations. Wide-eyed Lilus recounts her science lessons in a passage that humorously juxtaposes planets, poisonous mushrooms, weather systems, and angels with transparent wings, all on a par as equally valid topics for objective inquiry. And Mariana frequently interrupts her own enthusiastic, rapid-fire narration of boarding school camaraderie to reflect upon the things that she and her classmates did *not* discuss. Poverty, injustice, and class difference never enter the conversations or, presumably, the thoughts of the girls whose family names—de Bayle, Somoza, Ferré—guarantee their place at "the top of the top, la crème de la crème, la cereza en la punta" (99). The voice of an older, more critical Mariana is evident here behind her multilingual recitation of adolescent self-satisfaction and her dreams of movie stars and Milky Way bars.

Mariana's parroting of North American popular culture in the chapters that recall her years at the convent school demonstrates the impact of Hollywood and Broadway on her imagination. Cary Grant, Fred Astaire, and Judy Garland are the stuff of daydreams for wealthy Mexican, Nicaraguan, and North American teenagers alike, although the consequence of assimilating visions of life "somewhere over the rainbow" may be more disastrous for the young woman who will return to the reality of life in the

Third World. Back at home in Mexico City, Mariana confesses: "Dentro de mí hay una inmensa confusión y para escapar de ella, me la paso inventándome historias: soy la heroína de la película. Amanezco un día Ingrid Bergman . . . y al otro Joan Fontaine" (107).[26] Away from the imposed routine of the school she feels herself adrift, and it is clear that nothing in her education has prepared her to face change and to make decisions.

Mónica, the protagonist of "El limbo," one of Elena Poniatowska's best short stories, suffers from a similar inability to understand and react appropriately to the circumstances around her. In both "El limbo" and *La "Flor de Lis"* the main characters' adoption of the devalued languages of consumer culture and their assimilation of a banal Christianity contribute to their damaging misinterpretations of events and their conformity to the status quo.

Mónica, also the daughter of a wealthy family, is awakened one morning to brief rebellion by the shocking revelation of a servant's secret pregnancy and subsequent rejection of the newborn baby. Indignant in the face of everyone else's indifference, Mónica tries to take charge of the tiny life. But her capacity to assess either the servant's plight, the baby's needs, or her own egotistical motivations is severely hampered by the poverty of her world view. An avid reader of Nancy Drew mysteries, women's fashion magazines, and sensationalist newspapers, Mónica misreads the present crisis through the hackneyed vocabulary and the clichéd images of consumer society.[27] That is, she "sees" the world through a particularly distorted lens, and neither she nor the baby stands a chance of overcoming the injuries of ignorance. A trip to the hospital emergency room, for example, becomes a falsely heroic crusade against injustice in which the self-appointed heroine soon stumbles against the well-deserved skepticism and mistrust of the very people she had hoped to "help": the poor women who must wait long hours for inadequate care at the clinic. The infant's physical needs are merely the trigger for another frivolous fantasy, this one spun straight out of the pages of *American Baby* magazine. "¡Había un niño en la casa, un niño chiquitito! Se necesitaban pañales, camisitas, baberos, una almohada diminuta, una cobija con borregos pintados . . . allá el aceite y el algodón, todo limpio y blanco, imposible no conmoverse ante la pequeñez de las prendas."[28] The reader, however, quickly sees through Mónica's facile enthusiasm and perceives the enormous futility of her rescue mission. In fact, Mónica's rebellion lasts only a very few hours, and by day's end she has returned, safe and just a bit cynical, to her world of cocktail parties, embroidered tablecloths, and crystal lamps, "porque después de todo, la vida de uno es más fuerte que la de los demás" (because after all, your own life has a stronger claim than that of others).[29]

In both "El limbo" and La "Flor de Lis" Elena Poniatowska manipulates the clichéd vocabularies of Hollywood and popular literature to portray the precariousness of an identity constructed out of fundamentally debased materials. Mónica and Mariana internalize the ideologies of class and race privilege, feminine subordination, and consumer culture through the languages that they have absorbed, and their stories lead us to believe that they will continue to live out the mystifying fictions that those languages inscribe.

In La "Flor de Lis," then, the predominant focalization and narration through the eyes and the language of the young Mariana and the prevalence of the present tense are essential components of the novel's representation of female development. The story unfolds in consonance with the protagonist's limited but growing awareness of people and events and her relationship to them. Lack of distance and the emphasis on the lived moment are symptomatic of her incapacity for self-reflection and her inability to detect the discrepancies and contradictions inherent in her privileged status. The narrative scheme thus far described constructs an image of stunted growth, a search for self apparently thwarted by obedience and ignorance. But the choices of narrative perspective and time frame are only two elements, albeit important ones, of a complex text. In spite of Mariana's restricted powers of conscious self-reflection, through her close-up re-envisioning of her childhood she successfully records in sharp detail the very factors that threaten to blind her. That is, the novel presents a paradoxical situation. Mariana's unblinking eye often "sees" quite clearly (and focuses for the reader) the causes of her predicament, causes which her conscious "I" may not register or comprehend. The repeated use of the verb "to see" itself confirms the centrality of vision in the novel. With striking frequency Mariana narrates what she sees around her as opposed to what she herself does or says, suggesting her passive absorption of all manner of stimuli and alluding to the importance of "appearances" for upper-class women. But the crucial role of sight in the verbal self-portrait raises two even more fundamental questions. What image specifically does Mariana see—whether the object is present or absent? And *from what angle* does she view the object that she struggles to hold in her sights? The answers to these questions offer haunting testimony to a child's unanswered need for love and recognition.

WHAT THE EYE/I SEES:
THE BLINDING LIGHT OF LUZ

La veo salir de un ropero antiguo . . . (13)

El agua salada en los ojos. A través del agua la veo a ella, su sonrisa, su aire de distracción. Quisiera abrazarla. Se me deshace en espuma. (18)

De pronto la miro y ya no está. Vuelvo a mirarla, la define su ausencia. (42)[30]

At the visual and emotional center of La *"Flor de Lis"* dances the fleeting figure of Mariana's mother, Luz. She is the irresistible object of her daughter's anxious gaze and, equally, the light by which Mariana sees the world. Object and energy: Luz is the omnipresent absence, the empty, shifting place into which Mariana would invest her store of meaning by attempting to catch with words what was ever lovely to the eye but unreachable to the grasp. Mariana's relationship with her mother ties together the disjointed episodes and bridges both the structural and thematic gaps in the text. Around this pivotal relationship—cherished and flawed—turns Mariana's story of thwarted development.

Contemporary Western theories of individual development strive to explain the processes by which an infant acquires the sense of self and other that is integral to his/her life as a social being. The mother-child interaction, undeniably a critical factor in the baby's development, has been the target of innumerable competing interpretations. For my reading of the mother-daughter relationship as represented by the daughter in *La "Flor de Lis"* I have found valuable insights in the work of the North American feminist psychoanalyst Jessica Benjamin. Her 1988 book, *The Bonds of Love*, provides the theoretical underpinnings of my analysis of how Mariana envisions her mother and how she both sees and is blinded by the light of Luz. Benjamin focuses attention on the social dimension of human life in an effort to balance out (but not preclude) psychoanalysis' traditional emphasis on the intrapsychic and the unconscious, "the mind's private space." [31] Her study pays particular attention to the role of intersubjectivity, the experience of subject meeting subject, in human development. She hypothesizes that an individual's development of self distinct from and related to others depends on the interplay between one's internal psychic structures (the intrapsychic) and one's real relations with others (the intersubjective). Benjamin goes on to describe the "first bond" between mother and child (understanding mother in functional and not strictly biological terms) and the conflict between dependency and independence in infant life as a fundamental paradox: the paradox of experiencing connection and separation, self and other, simultaneously. She further suggests that a constant tension between assertion (of the self) and recognition (of the other as a person in his/her own right) is essential to the dual goal of autonomy and relatedness in human development. Because the child experiences greatest pleasure from what he/she accomplishes individually within a supportive social context, "assertion and recognition become the vital moves in the dialogue between self and other." [32] For the infant, the mother is the primary source of this kind of mutuality of recognition that encourages differentiation within attachment. [33]

I believe that all Elena Poniatowska's writing, fiction and nonfiction, inscribes these "vital moves" of assertion and recognition, moves played out in dialogue, public or private, real or imagined. The dialogue depends on a necessary balance between assertion and recognition, which may be more or less successfully maintained according to its context, as we have seen. *La "Flor de Lis"* presents an intimate view of the breakdown of the relational tension between Mariana and Luz, a breakdown that has a potentially devastating impact on the child's sense of self.

The passages quoted from the novel at the beginning of this section illustrate predominant motifs in Mariana's obsessive descriptions of her mother. The child's eye/I sees her mother, but the child is not herself seen. She is not recognized by the mother, who soon disappears from view. The mother's absence leaves a shadow—beautiful but intangible—on Mariana's eye, like the aftereffect of gazing into a blinding light. Luz's personality and the real conditions of Mariana's upbringing combine to deny her the nurturing mutuality of dependable interaction with a mother. Typically for an aristocratic European family of the 1930s and 1940s, Mariana and Sofía are raised by a succession of paid providers.[34] The little girls enjoy a delightful complicity with their first peasant nanny in France, but as the novel begins she is replaced by a severe governess, charged with instilling proper manners.

In Mexico Magda, an indigenous girl not so many years older than Mariana, is not only nanny and friend but also an indispensable link to Mexican customs and places for her two young charges. Grandmothers, too, play a role in caring for the younger generation, who will later live away from home at boarding school. But sudden dismissals and unannounced replacements thwart the child's need for continuity of attachment, and repeated experiences of abandonment skew Mariana's perception of herself and others. The beloved Nounou, attentive nurse and companion since Mariana's birth, is fired without warning when the protagonist is seven years old. Then wartime brings geographical dislocations, first within France and eventually across the sea to Mexico. Their governess accompanies the girls from Paris into the countryside but later disappears—left behind or called away?—and fades from memory. Magda also leaves Mexico City from time to time to visit her parents in the country, and although she always returns with a basket of fresh apples and new stories to share, after awhile she ceases to live in, and her ties to Mariana weaken.

Against this backdrop of moves and changes, their mother is also in constant motion, now in Paris, now at the countryside refuge, now rushing back to Paris without notice. Once in Mexico Luz is caught up in a social whirl that leaves little room for her young daughters. In addition to the turmoil of their situation or perhaps conditioned by it, Luz's emotional make-up, the "private space" of her psyche, is dominated by qualities of distraction, inattention, and self-absorption. Under stress, as when she must confront Jacques Teufel toward the end of the novel, Luz succumbs to illness, withdrawing even further from those around her. Boredom and a troubled marriage partially explain Luz's susceptibility to nervous attacks. But whatever the cause of her own somewhat precarious sense of self, Luz's behavior ignores her daughters' legitimate needs, and it conveys the message that only limited, negative means of control and self-determination are available to upper-class women in patriarchy.

Effectively excluded from the circle of her mother's concern, Mariana compensates for abandonment by creating and recreating a mental image of the absent mother. The lingering warmth of a rapid kiss, a sound of rustling skirts, a hint of perfume are the fragile traces of a presence that is defined by its absence. "La define su ausencia." Mariana's narration attempts to make present the absent mother, to fix and to possess with words an unattainable reality. If, in homage to a dream of beauty, Mariana emphasizes the visual in her descriptions, then the angle of her vision proves to be crucial to our interpretation of the image that she projects. Starting with the opening scene and continuing throughout the novel, Mariana locates herself at a distance from her mother, outside or beneath her notice. Peering from behind closed doors, waiting in the shadows, poised at the edge, or relegated to a corner, Mariana watches unseen, overlooked, and even, occasionally, stepped on by the very adults upon whom she depends for needed recognition. As we measure the angle of her sight in recurring scenes of exclusion and empty waiting, we can assess the failure of reciprocity between self and (m)other:

> Yo era una niña enamorada como loca. Una niña que aguarda horas enteras. Una niña como un perro. Una niña allí detenida entre dos puertas, sostenida por su amor. Una niña arriba de la escalera, esperando. Una niña junto a la ventana. El sólo verla, justificaba todas mis horas de esperanza. . . . jamás insistía yo frente a ella, pero sola, insistía en mi ilusión, la horadaba, le daba vueltas, la vestía . . . Eramos unas niñas desarraigadas, flotábamos en México, qué cuerdita tan frágil la nuestra. (47)[35]

How pervasive and consistent is the visual imagery with which the speaking I of Mariana recalls what her eye once strained to see. From the angle of her dependency, the child-focalizor remembers a figure always poised in flight, just out of reach. She utilizes the vocabulary of movement, water, body, and light to compose a study of her own insistent illusion. Mariana's mother lives in perpetual motion, her scarf flowing, her automobile pulling away from the house, and her voice ringing like a bell, lovely but distant. Even standing still, Luz trembles and sways, moved by the wind or by the beat of her pulse. "Revolotea, su vestido barre el suelo, pregunta a los cuatrovientos con sus ojos de cuatrovientos" (17). "Camina largo, no me oye, mamá, su vestido es el puro viento" (200).[36] Mariana knows herself incapable of slowing that inner impulse to flight which carries her mother away even when she seems to pause beside her daughter. But inaccessibility only intensifies the demand for recognition, still acute well into late adolescence. The seventeen-year-old Mariana stumbles against the child's unfulfilled need: "Mamá, mírame, estoy aquí . . . mamá no te vayas, cómo te detengo, no puedo asirte mamá" (Mama, look at me, here I am . . . don't go away, how can I stop you, I can't hold on to you) (200).

The association of the mother with water is another constant element in the novel's imagery. Sea, rain, and tears wash over her, restless waters which blur the outlines of her face and sting

Mariana's eyes. "Es mi mamá, sí, pero el agua de sal me impide fijarla, se disuelve, ondea, vuelve a alejarse" (Yes, it is my mother, but the saltwater blurs my vision, she dissolves in a wave, she moves off again) (29). Poniatowska calls upon the ancient association of the maternal with the creative and the destructive powers of the ocean in this sentence which dissolves mother and seascape into one vision of receding horizons. The destructive connotations of water predominate, as salt tears and sea spill, break, and corrode but do not nourish. Rain, too, is evoked not for its life-giving qualities but for the sad gray of overcast skies and the mingling of raindrops with tears on the mother's face.

In the eye of the beholder, an adoring and later a jealous Mariana, Luz embodies an idealized physical beauty. Mariana's fascination with her mother's body is again, in part, a measure of its radical unavailability. Caught in the off-balance dynamic of an unreturned gaze, Mariana contemplates her mother's beauty and sees the reflection of her own inferiority. "Dios mío, qué bonita es, qué bonita, nunca seré como ella, nunca. Incluso cuando sea vieja, su rostro será más bonito que el mío" (162).[37] If recognition is the essential response that encourages self-assertion, in its absence Mariana assumes an attitude of submissive veneration, never insisting, but never ceasing to wait. The psychic cost of a childhood lived lying in wait for and in the wake of the disappearing mother is therefore very high for the adolescent protagonist, who cannot separate from what was never sufficiently present to her.

The maternal body, although beautiful, is a fragmented body, always glimpsed in pieces. Hair, neck, legs, breasts, eyes: these are the shards of a broken mirror in which the protagonist cannot assemble her own whole self-image. They are also the signs through which Mariana inscribes the mother's body with a daughter's meanings and desires. Full, milk-white breasts, breasts like apples, signify both withheld nourishment and repressed sexuality. Bending down to kiss her little daughter good night, Luz's hair falls heavy and graceful as a tree branch but offers no support to the weight of Mariana's need. Equally telling are certain curious gaps in the narrator's memory. The fourteen-year-old

Mariana records not a single image of her mother pregnant with Fabián, whose birth is the cause of her definitive banishment. Luz's long, slender legs, compared to those of a deer, suggest graceful strength as well as fear and vulnerability. Mother and doe alike depend on flight to protect themselves from the very desire that their beauty arouses in others. The recourse of the gorgeously weak is not the confidence of assertion but the negativity of escape. Other descriptions hint further at Mariana's perception of her mother's fragility as a woman and her terrible vulnerability to the destructive power of men. In one startling passage Mariana observes "adivino sus pálpitos bajo la tela que no la protege, qué frágil se ve su nuca, con una sola mano, un hombre puede abarcarla sola, abarcar su cuello entero" (201).[38] Feminine beauty attracts and seduces, but it also inspires jealousy in other women, and it may bring harm from men to the woman who is powerless to control these effects on others.

Finally, Luz is light itself, but a dazzling light which does not illuminate, a brilliance which blinds the viewer and casts shadows. On the ship which takes them from Europe to America, from the familiar to the unknown, Mariana gropes in the darkness below deck: "La escalera desemboca en un estrecho pasillo y camino bajo el túnel; cuántos pasos hay que dar para llegar a la luz. Penden focos de luz amarilla pero yo quiero la luz del día" (29).[39] Above board, the reborn Mariana is blinded by the morning light and by the "descubrimiento deslumbrante" (dazzling discovery) of her mother standing at the prow, "volátil, a punto de desaparecer" (volatile, about to disappear) (29). "Deslumbrante," denoting both visual glare and cognitive confusion, perfectly captures Mariana's fascination with the light that blinds.

Without a doubt, the centrality of the mother, Luz, in *La "Flor de Lis"* structures the novel's portrayal of Mariana's stunted growth and lingering dependency. Mariana seems to be drawn, like a moth, perilously close to a consuming flame. But other characters also play significant and counter-balancing roles in the protagonist's search for identity and roots. As the story progresses other attachments begin to pull her gaze away from the mother's dazzling brilliance and out of her shadows by engaging her in new dialogues. The failure of that essential mutuality between mother and child conditions these alternative relationships and compromises growth, but our reading cannot discount the influence of many other characters in whom Mariana discovers pieces of her past and future selves.

Among the women who play a nurturing role in her life, Mariana feels a particular affection for the servants, an affection which harks back to her early bond with the French peasant nanny, Nounou. In Mexico, domestic servants provide needed connections to the new land and its people through the language they teach her and the places which they explore together by bus and on foot. The Zócalo, Xochimilco, Chapultepec, *tamalerías*, and innumerable city streets become sites of an encounter between the French-born *duquesita* and Mexican reality. The title of the novel celebrates the dual heritage, French and Mexican, that Mariana later claims. It is an obvious reference to the symbol of French nobility, and it is the name of a Mexico City *tamalería*, as documented by the menu that appears at the opening of the novel. Magda, hired by Luz at her daughters' insistence, comes to represent Mariana's idealized vision of the Mexican *pueblo* with her black braids, her fascinating tales and superstitions, and her generous indulgence of her young mistresses' whims. Magda is also the cause of Mariana's first pangs of social conscience. Their intimacy forces the girl to question a social hierarchy which separates the two friends at dinnertime, sending one to the kitchen and the other to the sumptuous dining room.

But Mariana's discomfort at this injustice is short-lived and limited to Magda as an individual. It does not translate into a generalized critique of the inequalities which inform so many aspects of her daily life. Later at the convent school she accepts the notion that the hierarchy of ranks among the sisters is based on each one's "natural" capacity: "Hay unos que nacieron para servir a otros y sansiacabó" (Some people were born to serve others, and that's all there is to it) (104). Therefore, Mariana's affection for Magda and the kitchen workers at school, however sincerely experienced, does not move her to question the foundations of her own relative privilege. Nor does Mariana ask how the mutuality of affection which she celebrates may be compromised from both sides by the play of superiority and dependency, affection and domination, guilt and gratitude which supports the mistress-servant relationship.[40] Magda and others like her open Mariana's eyes to Mexico by offering her a glimpse of the city beyond the French quarter, but they remain the subordinate other, and Mariana cannot be expected to see her own future self truly reflected in their dark faces.

In Western patriarchal culture, identification with the father has traditionally provided the growing child with the means of entry into the outside world of work, public life, and public recognition. Again according to Jessica Benjamin, the girl-child, excluded by her father's insistence on his difference from her, may be disappointed in her search for a wider stage and a greater independence, and she may resolve that disappointment by retreating to home and mother, with their corresponding encouragement of dependency. For Mariana the classic scenario is complicated by the status of her father as a kind of "missing person." Literally missing in action during the war, Casimiro remains figuratively missing at home because he is disconnected from family life, and he proves to be ineffectual as well in the outside world of business and bureaucracy. Like Luz, Casimiro is defined by his absence. Mariana senses his distance and his incapacity to respond to her on the very first morning of his return from the war. "Se queda en la orilla. Así será siempre; se quedará en la orilla. . . . A papá lo quiero cuando me rehuye, cuando sus ojos son ese verdor de inseguridad y de expectación que después sabré que jamás se cumple, porque mi padre no conoce el camino, no sabe por dónde entrarle a la vida" (85).[41]

The reader learns little about Casimiro: only that his business dealings are shaky, he never plays to the end of a piece on the piano, and he rarely argues openly with Luz in spite of the evident tensions between them. He is notable primarily for how little space he occupies on the page or in the home, and he remains an enigma. Once again, Elena Poniatowska's short stories speak directly to the novel's silences. "De Gaulle en Minería" from *De noche vienes* portrays a character similar to Casimiro:

a decorated war hero living in Mexico with his wife and children. The story, an interior monologue narrated by a former officer in the French resistance, represents a leap of the imagination by the author into the thoughts of a man much like Casimiro and, in fact, much like Poniatowska's own father.[42]

In "De Gaulle en Minería" the retired French officer recalls wartime experiences as he waits in a receiving line at a banquet held in honor of his former general, now president of France. Fragments of a night spent in the trenches in Europe alternate with snatches of dialogue overheard at the elegant Mexico City party. Slowly, slowly the long night passed for the captain and his aide, Patitas, and slowly, too, he now moves down the long line of well-wishers. He had met de Gaulle once before in Africa, and over and over he rehearses what he will say to him tonight, only to find his thoughts slipping away as they used to do years before in sudden attacks of battlefield amnesia. The parallel stories resolve in parallel frustrations: the captain witnesses with horror a misdirected attack on civilians; and, now a civilian himself, he misses his long-awaited chance to pay homage to the great general when the receiving line is cut short. The dizzy spells that the narrator suffers during the noisy, crowded party are the symptoms of his disengagement from the present under the hold of painful, painfully private memories. In the closing lines of the story the narrator's past asserts its power over present reality. "Me introduzco de nuevo en mi lobera y pienso en mi fiel Patitas. ¿Dónde estará ahora?"[43]

I believe that in "De Gaulle en Minería" Poniatowska explores the very traumas that haunt Mariana's father, Casimiro, traumas which La "Flor de Lis" cannot divulge because it chooses to tell the daughter's story over the father's. Ultimately, neither Casimiro nor Luz "survives" for their children in the way required by Jessica Benjamin's concept of mutuality in intersubjectivity. However compelling the reasons for the parents' own vulnerability, the novel is concerned to record not primarily its causes but its effects on Mariana. The dialogue between parent and child, the vital moves of assertion and recognition, fail to hold, upsetting the delicate balance of their relationship. Casimiro's incomplete melodies and Luz's air of distraction are the nonresponses to which Mariana's voice futilely appeals and then futilely imitates. For at a crucial moment in the text, Mariana realizes that she has become her parents, especially her father, with his anguish and his unfinished tasks. Like him, she perches on a piano bench confident and accomplished in her playing, only to stop short of the end and change pieces, holding back until an ever-deferred tomorrow. Growing up in the shadows and held back by a fear of doors, Mariana's vision of herself and of others seems to be fatally governed by the blinding light of Luz.

THE HIGH PRICE OF PRIVILEGE

Beyond the debilitating experience of loss and longing for the mother so poignantly evoked in La "Flor de Lis," the novel demonstrates that Mariana's privileged class position sets up other kinds of obstacles to her growth and independence. Here and in Elena Poniatowska's other texts, privilege is shown to exact a high price from its beneficiaries, who, like Mariana, often remain largely unaware of the losses occasioned by their "gain." My own thinking about the high price of privilege in the writing of Elena Poniatowska has been prompted in part by the essay "Identity: Skin Blood Heart" by North American feminist Minnie Bruce Pratt. Pratt asks how and why an individual who benefits from certain class, race, and/or cultural privilege might be motivated to confront the complex origins and consequences of oppression. In a more radical manner than Poniatowska's novel, Pratt's autobiographical essay deconstructs the status of home, identity, community, and privilege as terms of safety and coherence. By examining history, personal experience, and the geography and architecture of the various "homes" that she herself has occupied, Minnie Bruce Pratt confronts fear and explains her own willingness to negotiate the risks inherent in seeking change. Her essay lays bare the false gains and the "'threatening' protection" afforded to the few by the oppression of the many.[44] While La "Flor de Lis" does not match Pratt's open engagement in social conflict and struggle, Minnie Bruce Pratt's essay helps to clarify certain elements in Elena Poniatowska's novelistic portrayal of a child of privilege.

As I have shown, the construction of Mariana as a child narrator-focalizor limits her overt participation in a critique of privilege. That is, her youthfulness and her proximity to her own circumstance frequently prevent Mariana from recognizing the contradictions within which she lives. Nevertheless, as I have also suggested, her acute eye provides a wealth of telling details that the reader may interpret at apparent cross-purposes to Mariana's intentions. Because we ourselves read as adults and not as children, we often see Mariana's version of an event as a kind of misreading on her part, an error caused by inexperience. Such discrepancies permit us to predict certain outcomes and to draw certain conclusions that exceed Mariana's view. Therefore, the text positions us as privileged readers, and our point of view is essential to deconstruct the irony of Mariana's naiveté. Additionally, our knowledge of Elena Poniatowska's other texts influences our reading of the novel, as we have seen with the examples of the short stories "El convento," "El limbo," and "De Gaulle en Minería." The deconstruction of class privilege in the novel therefore depends on the intertextual dialogue between the reader and a myriad of other writings.

The first part of the novel already defies an uncritical valorization of the domestic and social prerogatives enjoyed by the female members of the Mexican upper class. That is, in spite of Mariana's obvious admiration for her mother, Luz's limited range of action, her loss of authority in the home when Casimiro returns from the war, and the frivolity of her social life constitute a veiled indictment of privilege. The automobile provides Luz with one means of independence of movement, and her trips outside the city represent a single, self-contained rebellion against confinement. In contrast, her daily sacramental tending of the rose garden with water and knife assumes the significance of a religious ritual performed to sanctify an ideal of feminine beauty and enclosure. Luz, her sister Francisca, and their mother may be high priests in the sanctuary of the walled garden, but their hereditary power to feed and to prune serves purely ornamental ends. Luxury items themselves, the three women cultivate the fruits of their own futility. After describing this morning ritual in exquisite detail, Mariana lets drop a rare hint that she will one day reject the legacy of her female forebears. "A diferencia de las flores de mi bisabuela, de mi abuela, de mi madre, mi tía, las mías serán de papel. Pero ¿en dónde van a florear?" (86).[45] This allusion to a future as a writer fashioning paper flowers out of words suggests an incipient challenge to the nonprofessional, un-salaried status of Luz from the outwardly obedient, even rever-ential Mariana. The choice of paper flowers over real blooms also celebrates a deliberate, anti-aristocratic vulgarity of decor, suggesting that Mariana will shun the unproductive and debili-tating leisure of her mother's routine.

Material possessions exact another high price from the women who are privileged enough to own rich furnishings. Furniture, in particular, represents a double burden for Mariana and for the anonymous I narrator-protagonist of "El inventario" from the 1967 *Cuentos de Lilus Kikus*. Antique chairs, tables, and cabi-nets demand constant cleaning, polishing, and restoration, and even under the best of hands they eventually weaken with wear and rot. The protagonists of La *"Flor de Lis"* and "El inven-tario" live under the alienating weight of a European culture whose artifacts claim hegemony over their Mexican surround-ings. Nevertheless, submission to the power of inherited luxuries does offer as well its own seductive pleasures to the woman who lovingly gives her body to the strong arms, broad back, and smooth seat of polished wood. Furniture takes the place of ab-sent men in the two households, offering both material security and sexual gratification to women. Although the woman may believe that she herself possesses the furniture, the stories reveal her to be the captive of their needs and demands.

The anonymous narrator-protagonist of "El inventario" seems to take responsibility for her own future by making a clean break with the past. She stubbornly divests herself of family heirlooms, overcoming pangs of regret while packing them off into storage. But significantly, at the end of the story, she experiences tremen-dous fatigue and emptiness at their departure, and she begins to fear the consequences of her actions. The sight of the once cherished objects unceremoniously piled into moving vans provokes doubt, and there is no promise that the young woman will know how to enjoy her new freedom from family ties. In contrast, in La "Flor de Lis" Mariana defends the beauty of familiar luxuries against the ridicule dealt out by Thérèse Nissan and, later, by Jacques Teufel. Only in the final pages of the novel does she start to contemplate her own rebellion against the gem-incrusted bonds of love.

The principal voice for social change in La "Flor de Lis" belongs to the French priest, Jacques Teufel. By the time she meets him, Magda and the anonymous faces of the Mexico City populace have already awakened in Mariana a sentimental interest in her country's history and culture, particularly as lived by the indigenous peasantry. But as we have seen, Mariana's affections for the subordinate other do not immediately translate into a critique of class privilege. In contrast to the sweet, subdued voices of the oppressed in the novel, Teufel, backed by all the authority of the Church, France, and masculinity, articulates a scathing challenge to the self-satisfied complacency of his wealthy parishioners. Bursting onto the scene of privileged lassitude, his raw energy, crude manners, and shocking ideas about social class divisions and personal self-sacrifice immediately shake Mariana out of her stupor.

The narration of the three-day retreat which Mariana attends with other members of her scout group consumes forty pages, about one-sixth of the novel. The contradictory figure of Teufel, half demon and half avenging angel (his name is the German word for devil), fills Mariana's eyes even to the point of temporarily shutting out her mother's light. Virtually all the girls at the retreat are similarly fascinated by him. He simultaneously attracts, confuses, and disturbs them with his burning gaze and his calls to social justice and personal liberation. "Algo pide, ¿pero qué? Estamos dispuestas a dárselo, pero ¿qué es lo que quiere?" (134).[46] He is Cary Grant and Jesus Christ, a priest with hawk eyes and a voice like a cave ready to swallow up innocent young "niñas de bien." When the retreat is over, Teufel comes to live at Mariana's home, where he strengthens his influence over her and successfully courts Luz into his camp. Now competing with Luz for the father's attentions, Mariana's love for her beautiful mother becomes tinged with jealousy.

The encounter with Teufel is a decisive event, with both positive and negative consequences for Mariana's development, and these episodes further highlight the crucial role of the reader in deconstructing privilege in the novel. Teufel opens Mariana's eyes to some of the economic and cultural inequities of contemporary Mexican society. Against her tendency to indecision and procrastination, he seems to offer purpose and meaning through commitment to social action. Frequently invited to dine at the homes of the most influential families, he embodies a healthy defiance of the labyrinthine etiquette of polite conversation and intricate silver place settings. But Mariana's admiring descriptions of the priest also reveal troubling hints of emotional instability, and his revolutionary rhetoric rings increasingly false to the reader's ears.

Again, the narrator faithfully records information which she is incapable of interpreting as prejudicial to the object of her love. The reader, on the other hand, is bound by no such loyalty. A telling incident occurs when Sofía flirts with one of her father's employees, and Teufel, the social revolutionary, angrily denounces her for unseemly behavior in front of a social inferior. Although Mariana perceives an inconsistency between this exaggerated reaction and Teufel's previous messages of social equality, the protagonist is largely upset because Sofía and not she was the motive for this obvious attack of jealousy. The reader, in turn, uses Mariana's own words as evidence against her interpretation of events, substituting our judgments for her mistakes. Sofía's nightmares, the revealing entries in a diary that Luz keeps, and Mariana's growing resentment and confusion after this episode reflect the building tensions that threaten to splinter the family. And so ultimately Mariana alone is shocked by reports of Teufel's crazed behavior on a youth group hike, the revelations of his womanizing, and his dismissal from the parish. The disjunction between Mariana's misreadings and our reading challenges the identity between reader and character which the prevailing focalization fosters, and it contributes significantly to the portrayal of Mariana's naiveté.

Jacques Teufel's occupation of the pavilion behind Mariana's home introduces an element of danger into the secure sphere of domestic life. Ironically, Casimiro himself invites the father to inhabit the quintessentially feminine space of his wife's garden, thus wielding patriarchal prerogative in a gesture which only underscores his lack of real authority in the home. Mariana strives to serve the priest in every way possible: she brings him his breakfast, dials his phone calls, and generally makes herself available to do his bidding. Once more, far from affording protection, submission to another's will threatens individual integrity. One evening, after Teufel has begun to show the signs of his emotional illness in numerous outbreaks of fury, he cruelly and obscenely ridicules Mariana over a trivial remark that she makes. When he stalks away, Mariana remains alone in the garden, now a violated space adorned by "rosales inútiles y el rocío que va desapareciendo" (useless rosebushes and the evaporating dew) (195). Neither feminine self-sacrifice nor the once glorious roses have any power to shield Mariana from Teufel's anger. Home, constructed upon hierarchical and exclusionary practices, is a site of danger for woman, who draws an equivocal benefit from what Minnie Bruce Pratt rightly calls its "threatening protection."

Jacques Teufel's lasting impact on Mariana, then, does not stem primarily from his social message, which does contain some positive elements. Clearly, for all that he is correct in challenging the social and sexual mores of his parishioners, his manipulative and *machista* posturing diminishes the authority of his call to action and personal freedom. Playing off woman against woman, even daughter against mother, Teufel betrays their trust.[47] The shock effect of his betrayal—painful and salutary—is the catalyst for Mariana's most significant, even if still uncertain, consciousness-raising. Minnie Bruce Pratt acknowledges that the key to leaving home, to risking a break with the familiar and the familial, may have to come from an experience of pain and conflict. For Pratt, growing up white, Christian, and female in Alabama in the 1950s, it was racial violence and her own lesbianism which forced her to examine the dangerously appealing notions of home as refuge and privilege as gain. Once "exposed" to the weapons of racism and homophobia, Pratt begins to cut through the multiple ideological obstacles to a recognition of injustice and responsibility for change. Mariana's confrontation with her own position of privilege occurs late in the novel, in large part as a result of Teufel's abandonment. Given the book's open-ended conclusion, we cannot say whether or not Mariana will "leave home" soon or ever, but events have conspired to undermine the security of home and the certainty of her future as a daughter of privilege. The insuperable absence of maternal recognition, the contact at home with servants and the pangs of conscience that their treatment provokes, and Teufel's mixed message of justice and betrayal combine to inflict an unfathomable pain.

In the final pages of the novel, Mariana meditates on the lessons of that pain. Confused and angry, she takes a first tentative step toward examining her inheritance and, in the process, toward distancing herself from it. In the mirror of her grandmother's and her mother's lives, Mariana sees the face of her own future loneliness, foreignness, fragility, and uncertainty. Closing her eyes, she sees the shadow of her younger self, unconscious and innocent; guilty, perhaps, of innocence. And she wants to flee from both of the frightening images, or to ward them off with incantations: "¡Váyanse al diablo, vuelvan al fondo del espejo . . . ! Váyanse hermanas en la desgracia, lárguense con sus peinetas de diamantes y sus cabellos cepillados cien veces, yo no quiero que mis ideas se amansen bajo sus cepillos de marfil y heráldicas incrustadas" (260).[48]

Jacques Teufel may have served as a catalyst for new ways of seeing the world, but Mariana will have to seek other sources of knowledge and identity to move through her pain and beyond it. Around her lies Mexico City, the "umbilical of the world," Mexican motherland, mother of sun/light. In dialogue across the immense space of the city, Mariana will seek a response to the question that she asks her mother and herself: "La tristeza que siento, ¿ésa dónde la pongo?" (The sadness that I feel, where do I put it?) (261). The sorrow of cultural uprootedness, of nonrecognition, of the unreturned gaze may heal under the warmth of the Mexican landscape and the Mexican tongue. "Mi país es esta banca de piedra desde la cual miro el mediodía, mi país es esta lentitud al sol" (261).[49]

CONCLUSIONS

La "Flor de Lis" is a courageous book for engaging in an intimate dialogue with the voices and the silences of female childhood. Elena Poniatowska's novel portrays the mother-daughter relationship with an intensity and poignancy that strike deep chords in her readers.[50] In concluding, one more voice joins the reading dialogue that I have carried out with La "Flor de Lis." Of Woman Born, Adrienne Rich's shattering meditation on "motherhood as experience and institution," collides with the words and the vision of Elena Poniatowska's Mariana to produce sparks of recognition across cultures. I would suggest that in its depiction of Mariana and Luz, La "Flor de Lis" offers a concrete and particularized version of what Rich describes as the terrible ambivalence—love, anger, rivalry, desire, rejection—that the daughter feels for the mother in patriarchy. Consider this passage from Of Woman Born: "Few women growing up in patriarchal society can feel mothered enough; the power of our mothers, whatever their love for us and their struggles on our behalf, is too restricted. And it is the mother through whom patriarchy early teaches the small female her proper expectations."[51]

Clearly Mariana cannot feel mothered enough by a woman whose distraction, distance, and vulnerability testify to her own troubled response to the restrictions of patriarchy's "proper expectations." Feeling herself abandoned, Mariana, like Adrienne Rich, speaks simultaneously of her rejection by and her desire for her mother. The novel is a testimony to "the ancient, unpurged *anger* of the child" and to the girl-child's persistent "*longing* for a woman's nurture, tenderness and approval, a woman's power exerted in our defense."[52]

Of Woman Born realizes a complex and comprehensive critique of the historical and cultural groundings of motherhood in Western society. The work of a poet and an essayist, a mother, a lesbian, and a feminist, the book engages "personal experience" and exhaustive research to begin to tell, among other tales, "the great unwritten story of mothers and daughters."[53] Not content to stop at the limits of rational understanding and forgiveness, Adrienne Rich proposes further that daughters need a double vision of their mothers in order to see them clearly and to transform anger and loss into strength. First we must see the absent mother through a child's eyes and needs, and then we must look beyond the individual mother to the cultural pressures that distort mothering and nurturance. True to its choice of a child-narrator, La "Flor de Lis" emphasizes the first step of this double vision over the second, more analytical one by representing as directly as possible the child's sense of loss. But, as I hope to have shown, an attentive reading of the novel recognizes the ironic, double-voiced potential of Mariana's narration as our words cross with hers, across the page.

Writing openly about her own childhood and her formation as a writer in the essay "A Question Mark Engraved on My Eyelids," Elena Poniatowska makes the following remark: "I dutifully accepted the repressive atmosphere, even though inside myself I sensed something subversive that I would have to let out: a joy at daybreak, as if a sun were going to burst from my mouth. But when? How?"[54]

The texts that I have studied in this book tell us much about how Elena Poniatowska's subversive tongue has burst the constraints of silence for herself and for others. In the early interviews and the stories of Lilus Kikus, dialogue and autobiographical reflection permitted the young writer to initiate a limited but significant challenge to her conservative upbringing. Elena Poniatowska's relationship with Josefina Bórquez, which remains inextricably tied to her creation of Jesusa Palancares, brought into sharp focus social class divisions and the numbing violence of poverty, while also validating the author's desire to belong to Mexico. No longer a "foreigner" but an increasingly dissident insider in Mexican journalism, Poniatowska's meticulous editing of the multiple perspectives recorded in La noche de Tlatelolco demonstrates her commitment to a responsible and responsive use of discursive authority on behalf of the silenced protagonists of 1968. Finally, La *"Flor de Lis"* presents her readers with a more intimate view of individual development and intersubjectivity, suggesting a potential for change in those persons whose privileged position would seem to imply a particularly high investment in the status quo. In all these works, Elena Poniatowska's cultivation of a dialogic creative process and a dialogic literary language makes possible an ever-renewed connection, imperfect but praiseworthy, across the abyss that separates self and other. Mariana of La *"Flor de Lis"* affirms the need to feel herself immersed in the pulsing life and light of her city. "Mi país es esta banca de piedra desde la cual miro el mediodía, mi país es esta lentitud al sol" (261). So it is also for Elena Poniatowska: on the sun-drenched stone bench, in the midst of the crushing din of Mexico City, she engages in the dialogues, the "crossed words," that continue to nourish her writing.

NOTES

INTRODUCTION

1. From an unpublished interview with Elena Poniatowska, June 1991. My translation from the Spanish. All further references to this interview will also appear translated directly into English.

2. Stanislaus Poniatowski reigned as king of Poland from 1764 to 1795. Juan Poniatowski, Elena's father, died in 1979.

3. Bakhtin, *Problems of Dostoevsky's Poetics*, 151.

4. Ibid.

5. Ibid., 368–369.

6. Ibid., 4.

7. Kostakowsky, "La entrevistadora."

8. Elena Poniatowska's major new work, *Tinísima*, was published after I had largely completed work on this study. *Tinísima* represents an important landmark in Elena Poniatowska's writing, and the analyses that I have carried out here lay the groundwork for appreciating the new novel's elaboration of the writer's predominant thematic and formal concerns: the cultural outsider, feminism, class consciousness, social and political activism, and the blending of documentary and invented material into a seamless narrative whole.

1. FACE TO FACE

1. Luis Spota used this phrase to describe his own experience in a statement that fits Elena Poniatowska equally well. "It is in the tumult of chasing the news that one acquires the necessary discipline, the con-

sistency, the sensitivity to see and understand and the aptitude for personal sacrifice which literary creation demands" (*Los narradores ante el público*, 75–76, my translation). Here as throughout the book I have translated Spanish language material from Elena Poniatowska's writing and from other sources whenever a published English translation does not already exist. As a rule, when quoting passages from the texts by Poniatowska which I am analyzing, I have given the Spanish language original in the body of the chapters and I have put the translation into an endnote (or, if a very short phrase, in parentheses immediately following the quote). However, when quoting from interviews, articles, and other critical sources I have translated directly into English in order to eliminate unnecessary repetition. When published translations of Elena Poniatowska's works are available, I utilize the English version in the body of the text and document the source.

2. Elena Poniatowska's published interviews have received remarkably little critical attention. In the only article that I have seen which analyzes the interviews exclusively, Janet N. Gold studies the problem of authenticity in *Palabras cruzadas* and *Domingo siete*. See Gold, "Elena Poniatowska."

3. See the prologue to Carlos Monsiváis' anthology of the Mexican chronicle, *A ustedes les consta*.

4. See Merrill, *Handbook of the Foreign Press*, 284–290.

5. In her 1983 study of Mexican political journalism, Petra María Secanella confirms the continuing dependence of the national press on the interests of those in power throughout the 1960s and 1970s, at the same time that she gives credit to the more independent stance taken by some notable journalists and newspapers, including Salvador Novo, Carlos Monsiváis, Julio Scherer García, Manuel Buendía, and Elena Poniatowska; and *Excélsior* (1968–1976), *Unomásuno*, and *Proceso* (Secanella, *El periodismo político en México*).

6. Ruiz Castañeda, "La mujer mexicana."

7. Ibid., 221.

8. Elena Poniatowska with Beth E. Jörgensen, June 1982.

9. The articles of *Palabras cruzadas* are based on interviews with the following people: Alfonso Reyes, Lázaro Cárdenas, Diego Rivera, Alfonso Caso, María Lombardo de Caso, Carlos Pellicer, David Alfaro Siqueiros, Juan Rulfo, Carlos Chávez, François Mauriac, Luis Buñuel, Cesare Zavattini, Alejo Carpentier, and Pablo Casals.

10. Elena Poniatowska in an interview with Beth Miller, *Veinte y seis autoras del México actual*, 316.

11. Kostakowsky, "La entrevistadora," 5.

12. "Have you read some of my works?"

"No, Mr. Mauriac. I've only just started. Yesterday I bought *Serpent's Nest* . . . But tell me, which is your best book?"

"There is no point in my answering, Miss, you don't know my thought. This conversation is impossible . . ."

13. François Mauriac, tall and thin, began to rub his hands together impatiently, under the pretext that it was cold in his library.

14. De Lauretis, *Alice Doesn't*, 3.

15. Bakhtin, *Dialogic Imagination*, 284.

16. Among the most outstanding examples of the exploration of the face/mask theme since colonial times are Juan Ruiz de Alarcón's *La verdad sospechosa*, Rodolfo Usigli's *El gesticulador*, Octavio Paz's *Labyrinth of Solitude*, and Carlos Fuentes' *Todos los gatos son pardos*.

17. The four sources for the testimonies are Guadalupe Marín, Diego Rivera's first wife, their daughters, Lupe and Ruth, and his friend and fellow artist, Doctor Atl.

18. . . . humanity is woman. We men are a subspecies of animals, almost stupid, insensitive, completely inadequate for love, created by women to serve them.

19. The real Poles are the ones in Poland, . . . the ones that make up the people, that is, workers and peasants, and not the ones that are here in Mexico doing their little interviews.

20. See Paul Smith, *Discerning the Subject*.

21. . . . who at times is reserved among men, or even severe in his opinions . . . in the presence of women shows nothing but tenderness.

22. And no way were he and Manuelita going to carry them, like those little Indians one sees walking along the highway carting their heavy pots of maguey juice.

23. García Flores, "Entrevista," 29.

24. When I give the matter careful thought, most illustrious Queen . . . I come to one certain conclusion: language was ever the companion of empire, and so closely followed in its footsteps that together they began, grew and flourished, and afterward together they both fell (Nebrija, *Gramática*, 97). Nebrija's grammar was the first written grammar of a romance language.

25. García Pinto, "Entrevista," 180.

26. Juan Bruce-Novoa detects what he calls the "feminist origins of commitment," commitment, that is, to social change, in the stories of *Lilus Kikus*, published in 1954. Without endorsing his analysis and conclusions here, I do want to suggest that the autobiographical narrative of *Lilus Kikus* offered the young Elena Poniatowska a less constrained site for writing, and therefore the stories may indeed express the critical engagement with "female concerns" that Bruce-Novoa defines. The

writing of "fiction" and "journalism" are simultaneous and intertwined activities throughout Elena Poniatowska's career. I chose to focus on her early interviews in this first chapter because of her prominence as an interviewer and her continuing use of interview techniques in the production of texts, and as a way of asking what potential that practice held for her for posing a challenge to dominant discourse at a specific moment of her career (Bruce-Novoa, "The Feminist Origins of Commitment").

27. Steele, "Entrevista," 90.

28. Lorde, "Master's Tools," 112.

2. CREATIVE CONFUSIONS

1. *Hasta no verte Jesús mío* has been translated into English by Magda Bogin, although that translation has never been published. She renders the title into English as "Here's Looking at You, Jesus." Elena Poniatowska explains that the phrase used in the title comes from a traditional toast exhorting drinking companions to empty their glasses. She chose it for her novel because of her protagonist's drinking habits.

2. Part of the controversy to which I allude centers precisely on the status of *Hasta no verte Jesús mío* as Elena Poniatowska's "first novel." Some readers consider *Lilus Kikus*, published fifteen years earlier, to be a novel, although the 1954 text was reissued in 1967 as *Los cuentos de Lilus Kikus* along with other short stories by the author. It is also possible to defend that *Hasta no verte Jesús mío* is not a novel at all but a *testimonio* along the lines of Elizabeth Burgos and Rigoberta Menchú's *Me llamo Rigoberta Menchú y así me nació la conciencia* and Moema Viezzer and Domitila Barrios de Chungara's *Si me permiten hablar: Testimonio de Domitila, una mujer de las minas de Bolivia*. It is widely acknowledged that many of Elena Poniatowska's books straddle the line between fiction and nonfiction; novel, novella, and short story; and novel and biography, throwing conventional literary classifications into a healthy state of confusion.

3. *Hasta no verte Jesús mío* is Poniatowska's most widely translated book as well, having appeared in French, Polish, German, Dutch, and Italian translations. The publication of an English translation has unfortunately been stalled for many years.

4. In the first part of the study I refer to the book as a novel and I employ methods of analysis usually associated with fictional texts. In the later, more "contextual" sections of the chapter I discuss the ques-

tion of assigning any single classification (i.e., novel, testimony) to the book.

5. Hancock, "*Hasta no verte Jesús mío:* Una heroína liberada"; Tatum, "Elena Poniatowska's *Hasta no verte Jesús mío*."

6. Charles Tatum concludes that Jesusa ends up her life as a defeated revolutionary due to her ties to the "fanatical religious sect," the Obra Espiritual. Joel Hancock, on the other hand, holds the opposite view, as the title of his 1982 article shows: "*Hasta no verte Jesús mío:* Una heroína liberada." This article was also published in English in 1983 under the title "Elena Poniatowska's *Hasta no verte Jesús mío:* The Remaking of the Image of Woman." I will have occasion in my analysis to contest both critics' conclusions.

7. See Lemaître, "Jesusa Palancares"; Jaén, "La neopicaresca"; Friedman, "The Marginated Narrator"; Pérez Pisonero, "Jesusa Palancares"; Kushigian, "Transgresión"; and González-Lee, "Jesusa Palancares."

8. See Genette, *Narrative Discourse.*

9. Genette argues convincingly for discarding the traditional distinction between first-person narration and third-person narration. He affirms that all narrative texts are necessarily delivered by a first person, an I-narrator who may intervene at any time in the narration or who may remain hidden (ibid., 245).

10. The narrative situation just described corresponds to what Dorrit Cohn calls "dissonant self-narration" in her study of first-person narratives, *Transparent Minds* (145).

11. Smith, *Discerning the Subject*, xxx.

12. This is the third time that I have returned to the earth, but I had never suffered so much as in this reincarnation, because previously I was a queen. I know this because I saw my train in a vision. I was in a beauty shop with long, floor-length mirrors, and in one of them I saw my gown and its train.

13. Genette, *Narrative Discourse*, 222–223.

14. My father tried to keep him away from bad company, *as I did with Perico,* but in spite of everything he always hooked up with them. So they say, once a fool always a fool.

15. Genette, *Narrative Discourse*, 67.

16. Cohn, *Transparent Minds*, 148.

17. Cynthia Steele's excellent article, "Testimonio y autor/idad en *Hasta no verte Jesús mío* de Elena Poniatowska," appeared after I had completed work on this chapter. Steele explores the relationship between Felipe Palancares and Jesusa in considerable depth, explaining the daughter's dependency on her father in social as well as psychological

terms (see 162–165). Steele expands on her analysis of *Hasta no verte Jesús mío* in her recent book *Politics, Gender, and the Mexican Novel, 1968–1988*, which I received when my manuscript was undergoing final editing.

18. I slept on the floor behind a stove. After all, I was crashing and I had to sleep in the entry with the dog. They say that corpses and freeloaders soon stink. If I had no money, how could I eat? And why should they give me food if they didn't owe me anything? They did enough by giving me a corner to sleep in amidst their own poverty. No, there's no goodness in the world, nobody is any good, you mustn't believe in goodness.

19. I was a real tomboy, and I always liked to play at war, rock throwing, penny pitching, tops, marble shooting, wrestling, kicking, pure boys' stuff, stoning lizards to death and smashing iguanas against the rocks. . . . We used to hollow out a long reed, like a blowgun, and hunt with it. It didn't bother me to hurt the poor animals. Why should it? We all have to die sooner or later. I can't understand the way I was when I was little.

20. I wasn't pretty, far from it. . . . On the contrary, I just wanted to act like a man, pin up my hair, carouse with the boys, sing with the guitar.

21. Men are always abusive. As if that's what it meant to be a man. That's the sickness of Mexican men, believing that they're real cowboys because they ride on top of us.

22. See Salas, *Soldaderas in the Mexican Military*, especially chap. 3, "Amazons and Wives," for background on the participation of Mexican *soldaderas* in the 1910 Revolution.

23. When I was little I was dirty and lice-ridden, but with my husband my head was infested. He beat me and split open my scalp, and with the wounds and the blood my head was covered with ulcers and my long, wavy hair fell out. My scalp was crusty with filth, and it stayed that way because I couldn't bathe or change my clothes.

24. So I was a martyr. Not anymore I'm not. Sure, I suffer like everyone else, but not the way I suffered when I had a husband.

25. I stood looking at him. I didn't stoop and I answered him. "Fine. We'll kill each other because there's two of us here and I'm not the only one who's going to die. Get ready to defend yourself, because I'm ready." I don't know where I got such courage, I think from desperation, and I take out my pistol, but just then he got scared. I saw clearly how scared he was.

26. But afterwards I'm the one who got stubborn. Even as a child I was naturally bad. I was born mean, but Pedro never gave me a chance. The blessed revolution helped me grow up. . . . If I weren't so bad I

would have given in to Pedro till he killed me. . . . Later I said I wouldn't give in anymore, and I didn't. So much so that here I am today.

27. Monique Lemaître cites the importance of *no dejarse* as a common denominator linking a small group of female protagonists in Mexican literature published before 1970 ("Jesusa Palancares," 131–132).

28. I think that there must be a place right in hell for all the women who give in. Hot coals in their britches!

29. See Steele, "Testimonio," 173–177 for extremely interesting and pertinent background on *espiritualismo* and *espiritismo* in Mexico.

30. Charles Tatum concludes his article with the following statement. "The novel, set against the backdrop of the Revolution and the subsequent chaos, chronicles the defeat of a revolutionary—Jesusa—not an ideological or social defeat but one more absolute: a spiritual one" ("Elena Poniatowska's," 58).

31. In the chapter "Rewriting the Family" of her book *Plotting Women*, Jean Franco also discusses the ways in which Jesusa Palancares fails to fit into conventional gender categories, and Franco makes the interesting point that the belief in reincarnation itself undercuts the notion of fixed identity. See Franco, *Plotting Women*, esp. 179–180.

32. I've never liked children. They're a nuisance and evil./That boy's name was Rufino. He was already grown. He was like all kids. What's nice about them? They're a walking calamity.

33. One day you won't find me here, just the wind. That day will come and when it does nobody will be able to explain what happened. And you will think that everything has been a lie. It is true, it's a lie that we are here, . . . and a lie that you will miss me. If I'm not good for anything anymore, who the hell is going to miss me? Not at the shop either. Who do you want to miss me if I'm not even going to say goodbye?

Fuck off. Get out of here. Let me sleep.

34. But he came back penniless, shafted, and what for? It couldn't be more obvious. Don't be a damned fool, don't kid yourself. Look at me, I'm the one who feels bad when you spout out that drivel about people being good and caring about you.

35. In chapter 3 I discuss the concept of Latin American testimonial literature in more depth. There I focus on Elena Poniatowska's *La noche de Tlatelolco*, a classic example of the *testimonio*'s recuperation of "other histories" through oral history and documentary techniques.

36. I have recently read Richard Cándida Smith's review essay on Elena Poniatowska, written for the *Oral History Review*. Smith briefly addresses this same point in his analysis of *Hasta no verte Jesús mío* (see Smith, "¿Quien quiere?" 77).

37. I quote throughout from the English version of the essay, referring to it as "Here's to You" followed by the corresponding page number.

38. See also Steele, "Testimonio," for her research into the transcriptions that Elena Poniatowska made from her interviews with Jesusa Palancares.

39. Poniatowska, "Testimonios," 33–35.

40. Poniatowska, *Ay vida*, 193.

41. René Jara suggests that even while denying any claim that *testimonios* unproblematically capture historical reality, it is important to recognize the "traces" of a history which would otherwise be completely lost to memory ("Prólogo," 2). John Beverley takes up Jara's idea to explain that the particular "reality effect" of testimonial literature exists in that "it produces if not the real then certainly a sensation of *experiencing the real*" with "determinate effects on the reader that are different from those produced by even the most realist or 'documentary' fiction" ("Margin," 22).

42. Kerr, "Gestures of Authorship," 379.

43. Weil, "Human Personality," 73, my emphasis.

44. Ibid., 85.

45. Jesusa exists, that's true. She is a flesh and blood person . . . For everybody else, Jesusa is a poor old woman who says the same strange, tedious things over and over to the point of boredom. . . . Complain, complain, Jesusa is just like many old people; those who move along the sidewalk, hugging the wall, and *whom we instinctively avoid because they slow us down* and we are always in a hurry ("Un libro que me fue dado," 3–4, my emphasis).

46. Cynthia Steele also examines these tensions, highlighting the sense of guilt which Poniatowska often expresses and making important connections between Elena Poniatowska and Rosario Castellanos in this regard (see, for example, Steele, "La mediación").

47. Stacey, "Can There Be a Feminist Ethnography?" 111.

48. In the 1978 *Vuelta* essay, as on many other occasions, Elena Poniatowska explains Bórquez's opposition to the tape recorder: it robbed electricity that Bórquez could scarcely afford, it took up too much space in the tiny room, and it was a borrowed machine which Poniatowska was foolish to carry with her.

49. "Jesusa's language is a composite of that of all the people I have known since childhood, because it contains popular expressions from many parts of the country" (Poniatowska, "Micrófono," 159, my translation). "I invented situations, I invented people. I speeded up some of the situations to make them more novelistic. And the very way in which I constructed the novel is different from what she told me" (Steele, "Entrevista," 94, my translation).

50. I refer here to a manuscript version of this essay which Elena Poniatowska generously made available to me.

51. Poniatowska, "Literatura testimonial," 3.
52. Ibid., 22.
53. Spivak, "Can the Subaltern Speak?" 295.
54. Poniatowska, "Question Mark," 90–91.
55. Ibid., 88.
56. Patai, "U.S. Academics," 149–150.
57. Steele, "Entrevista," 94, my translation.
58. Poniatowska, "Presentación," 76.
59. Weil, "Human Personality," 87.

3. CHRONICLES OF THE CONQUERED

1. García Flores, "Entrevista," 4.

2. Testimonial literature presents the reader with previously unrecorded or undocumented perspectives on contemporary Latin American society. Some of the urgent situations treated from the point of view of the oppressed and the marginalized in testimonial literature of the past twenty years include the labor movement among Bolivian mine workers, the "disappearance" of civilians in Chile, Argentina, and Mexico, the repression against indigenous populations in Guatemala, the Sandinista revolution in Nicaragua, guerrilla warfare in El Salvador, and the aftermath of the 1985 earthquake in Mexico City.

3. The problem of terminology is acute, as the following list of terms used by critics shows: *novela testimonio*, documentary narrative, documentary novel, *novela de no ficción, novela periodística*, narrative documentary prose, *crónica documental, género testimonio, testimonio, novela sin ficción*. These terms are not used in an entirely interchangeable fashion, although a single text may be classified in a number of different ways. *Testimonio* and testimonial literature are the two most widely used terms to designate a whole group of structurally and thematically diverse texts.

4. *Biografía de un cimarrón* is the life story of a former slave in Cuba who recounted his experiences to Cuban ethnographer Miguel Barnet. Barnet is himself one of the foremost practitioners of a certain kind of ethnographic *testimonio*, and he has written extensively about the process and the meaning of its production. *Me llamo Rigoberta Menchú* relates the life of a Quiché Indian woman of Guatemala and the traditions of her community, against a searing account of the terrible repression and violence perpetrated by the Guatemalan armed forces during the counter-insurgency campaign of the 1970s and 1980s. Rigoberta Menchú won the 1992 Nobel Prize for Peace.

5. Steele, "Entrevista," 102.

6. Alicia Partnoy originally wrote *The Little School* in Spanish, but she immediately collaborated on the English translation for publication in the United States, where she now resides. *La escuelita* still has not been published in Argentina.

7. See Steele, "La mediación."

8. "Well, just put down Juan," as if by giving their name they're afraid of bothering us, of taking up a space and a time that isn't theirs, "just Juan" . . . As long as the majority exists only en masse (as "the people"), the poor won't have a voice. Strong is their silence (Poniatowska, *Fuerte*, 11).

9. An exact accounting of the number of protesters killed, wounded, and imprisoned has never been possible due to the government's refusal to conduct a complete investigation of the events. Mexican news reports at the time were careful to quote the number of soldiers killed and injured, but initially the most accurate estimate of the number of civilians killed was considered to be that based on an investigation carried out by a British newspaper, the *Guardian*. In his important essay *Posdata*, Octavio Paz quotes their conclusions that at least 325 people were killed and thousands injured (38). In a talk given in San Antonio, Texas, in April 1988, Elena Poniatowska spoke of hundreds of protesters killed on October 2, 1968.

10. Carlos Monsiváis, in an article written for the twentieth anniversary of the publication of *La noche de Tlatelolco*, describes the atmosphere of repression and fear following October 2, 1968. The mechanisms of government censorship of the media included bribes and outright threats against journalists. When that failed, the authorities silenced their few remaining critics by arresting them (Monsiváis, "A veinte años," 23).

11. See articles on Tlatelolco literature by Lanin Gyurko and Dolly Young.

12. See Paz, *Posdata*; Fuentes, *Tiempo mexicano*; Castellanos, "Memorial a Tlatelolco," included in Poniatowska's *La noche de Tlatelolco*; and Usigli, *Buenos días*.

13. One important example is Luis González de Alba's *Los días y los años*, written while he was in prison. Elena Poniatowska, who interviewed González de Alba for *La noche de Tlatelolco*, remembers receiving a copy of the manuscript which was smuggled out of prison.

14. Two books that I have seen defend the Díaz Ordaz regime and condemn the student movement: José Cabrera Parra, *Díaz Ordaz y el '68*, and Roberto Blanco Moheno, *Tlatelolco, historia de una infamia*. The other books listed below represent a variety of approaches and judgments about the movement, but all defend the basic motives and goals of the students. Essays: Fuentes, *Tiempo mexicano*; Paz, *Posdata*;

Revueltas, *México 68*. Chronicles and testimonies: Balam, *Tlatelolco*; Campos Lemus, *El otoño de la Revolución*; Mora, *Tlatelolco 1968*; Monsiváis, *Días de guardar*. Novels: Avilés Fabila, *El gran solitario de Palacio*; González de Alba, *Los días y los años*; Mendoza, *Con Él*; Spota, *La Plaza*. Drama: Usigli, *Buenos días*. Poetry: Jesús Arellano, Juan Carlos Becerra, Rosario Castellanos, and José Emilio Pacheco.

15. "The events of 1968 signified for Mexico a crisis of growth, transformation and consciousness only comparable to the . . . defining moments of our national life: Independence, Reform and Revolution" (Fuentes, *Tiempo*, 147).

16. Elena Poniatowska in an unpublished interview with Beth Jörgensen, June 1982.

17. The idea of an officially imposed and false sense of "return to normality" is a major theme of *Nada, nadie*, as well. Poniatowska again makes it clear that in a situation of crisis the Mexican government acts principally to maintain order and a semblance of normality, even to the extreme of refusing offers of needed aid from the outside.

18. June 1982 interview with Elena Poniatowska.

19. Zunilda Gertel speaks of the "deconstruction and reconstruction of fragmentary languages which an editorial voice recomposes" (58) in her comments on the creative and interpretive labor of the editor in *La noche de Tlatelolco*.

20. Barnet, "La novela testimonio," 288.

21. Christ, "Author as Editor," 79.

22. David W. Foster also refers to the "authorial presence" as being limited to "the not insignificant ordering of the material that we read" ("Latin American," 45–46).

23. Derrida, "The Parergon," 20.

24. Ibid., 24.

25. Foucault, "Intellectuals and Power," 209.

26. In the English translation these photographs are placed in the middle of the book between "Taking to the Streets" and "The Night of Tlatelolco."

27. I will quote directly from the published English translation, *Massacre in Mexico*, throughout this chapter, referring to it as *Massacre* with the corresponding page number in parentheses. However, because the original Spanish title is so significant to my analysis, I continue to speak of the text as *La noche de Tlatelolco* except when quoting directly from the translation.

28. Derrida, "The Parergon," 33.

29. Roses, "Entrevista," 63.

30. Prada Oropeza, "De lo testimonial," 9.

31. See *El texto de la novela*, 15.

32. Julia Kristeva goes on to say: "The novel incorporating carnivalesque structure is called *polyphonic*. Bakhtin's examples include Rabelais, Swift, and Dostoievski. We might also add the 'modern' novel of the twentieth century—Joyce, Proust, Kafka—while specifying that the modern polyphonic novel, although analogous in its status, where monologism is concerned, to dialogical novels of the past, is clearly marked off from them" ("Word," 71).

33. Ibid., 66.

34. In English the titles of the poems are "Defeat of the Mexícatl People," "The Final Days of Tenochtitlán," and "The Destruction of Tenochcas and Tlatelolcas." Hereafter cited in text as *Broken Spears*.

35. "Some of our warriors stationed themselves on the rooftops of the Quecholan district, which is near the entrance to the market place, and from there they hurled stones and fired arrows at the enemy" (*Broken Spears*, 110). "We all felt absolutely helpless. On the other side of the street, across the Paseo de la Reforma, I happened to see comrades—kids no more than twelve or thirteen or fourteen—trying to throw stones at the cops and the troops" (*Massacre*, 231).

36. In 1520, while Hernán Cortés was absent from Tenochtitlán, Captain Pedro Alvarado used a religious festival in the Templo Mayor as a ruse to lure unarmed Aztec nobles into an easily closed-off area where he and his men proceeded to slaughter them. In early October 1968, with the Olympics approaching, the student movement and the government had a kind of truce in effect. As a result, the peaceful rally at Tlatelolco ended with an announcement cancelling a potentially confrontational march to the Instituto Politécnico Nacional. This cancellation was a gesture made to avoid the possibility of violence, and the government's actions were therefore all the more shocking. Both the histories under consideration note that a large number of the victims (Aztecs and modern demonstrators) were wounded from behind while attempting to escape.

37. The Noche Triste, or "Night of Sorrows," is thus named by Spanish chroniclers of the conquest, as it was the night when indigenous soldiers routed Cortés' troops from Tenochtitlán, at great cost to both sides. From the Aztec point of view it could perhaps better be called the "Victorious Night."

38. "The Final Omen: At nightfall it began to rain, but it was more like a heavy dew than rain. Suddenly the omen appeared, blazing like a great bonfire in the sky" (*Broken Spears*, 116). "The dead bodies were lying there on the pavement, waiting to be taken away. I counted lots and lots of them from the window, about seventy-eight in all. They were piling them up there in the rain" (*Massacre*, 210). "At just about that same time, the drizzle that had already begun to fall suddenly turned

into a downpour. It was about seven o'clock by then, and it was raining cats and dogs" (*Massacre*, 251).

39. García Flores, "Entrevista," 27.

4. INTIMATE CONVERSATIONS

1. "I am always more interested in the other. For a long time now I have thought of myself as a kind of vehicle through which other voices pass and through which events show themselves. I am at the service of others." June 1991 interview with Elena Poniatowska.

2. Poniatowska, "Question," 93.

3. See Chevigny, "The Transformation of Privilege."

4. Several short stories in *De noche vienes* also feature male protagonists and lower-class women: "Las lavanderas," "Esperanza número equivocado," "Cine Prado," and "Métase mi Prieta entre el durmiente y el silbatazo." I am primarily interested in this chapter in examining Poniatowska's creation of characters who share her background and social position.

5. Bruce-Novoa, "Feminist Origins," 511–512.

6. Poniatowska, *Los cuentos*, 18.

7. They are available again in a new edition: *Lilus Kikus* (Mexico City: Era, 1989).

8. See "La jornada," "Canto quinto," and "La felicidad."

9. I am thinking especially of "Love Story," "El inventario," "Castillo en Francia," and "El limbo."

10. See Flori, "El mundo femenino de Marta Lynch y Elena Poniatowska" and "Visions of Women."

11. López-Negrete, "Con Elena Poniatowska," 18.

12. García Flores, "Entrevista," 26.

13. June 1991 interview with Elena Poniatowska.

14. The *Bildungsroman* emerges in the eighteenth century in Germany with the work *Wilhelm Meister's Apprenticeship* by Goethe. The traditional European *Bildungsroman* narrates the development of a protagonist, usually male, from infancy to maturity. The central theme is usually the search for identity and the individual's self-realization as an integrated member of society. Women appear as protagonists of novels of development with increasing frequency in the twentieth century. See the ground-breaking 1983 study *The Voyage In*, ed. Abel, Hirsch, and Langland.

15. In her 1990 article on *La "Flor de Lis"* Sara Poot Herrera also describes the relationship between the novel and one particular story, "El inventario," as a kind of dialogue.

16. The terms used to identify current thinking in the theory of autobiography come from two influential studies: Lejeune, *On Autobiography* (autobiographical pact and autobiography as a mode of reading), and Bruss, *Autobiographical Acts.*

17. Stanton, *Female Autograph*, 4.

18. Méndez-Faith, "Translation of an Interview," 71–72.

19. Price, "Elena Poniatowska," 235.

20. Belejack, "Enormously," 4.

21. Abel, Hirsch, and Langland, eds., *Voyage In*, 14.

22. Carol Gilligan's *In a Different Voice* is one of the earliest and best-known studies that suggest that female psychological development privileges interpersonal relationships over absolute individuation. Nancy Chodorow's *The Reproduction of Mothering* is another influential work in this regard.

23. I introduce the narratological term *focalizor* here for its utility in helping us distinguish among the three functions carried out by Mariana. As narrator, she is the principal speaking agent or subject of discourse. As focalizor she embodies the perspective from which characters and actions are viewed (we readers see through her eyes). As protagonist she is the agent of actions (and the object of our gaze). The illusion of identity among these three functions created by the shared name is particularly strong in *La "Flor de Lis,"* where present tense narration and the absence of extensive direct intervention by the narrator tend to erase their crucial differences. See Bal, *Narratology.*

24. I see her come out of an antique wardrobe: She wears a long, white nightgown and one of those nightcaps that you see in the illustrations of the "Biblioteca Rosa" of the countess of Ségur. Closing the door, my mother slams it on herself and pinches her nose. That fear of doors will never leave me. They are always bruising something, cutting me off, leaving me out.

25. Neither my sister nor I say a word. "Children should be seen and not heard," warns my grandmother Beth. . . . One noon my mother forgets to cut up the meat for Sofía and me.

26. Inside I feel an immense confusion and to escape it I pass the time daydreaming. I am the heroine of the movie. One morning I wake up Ingrid Bergman . . . and the next morning Joan Fontaine.

27. Mónica Flori briefly alludes to this aspect of the story "El limbo" when she says that the protagonist's "primera reacción es la de interpretar la situación por medio de la realidad ficticia de sus lecturas" ("Mundo femenino," 28).

28. A baby in the house, a little tiny baby! We needed diapers, little shirts, bibs, a tiny pillow, and a baby blanket . . . over there the oil and

the cotton balls, everything clean and white. Who wouldn't be touched by such sweet little clothing? (Poniatowska, *Los cuentos*, 52.)

29. Ibid., 65.

30. I see her come out of an antique wardrobe.

Salt water in my eyes. Through the water I see her smile, her distracted air. I would love to hug her. She dissolves into foam.

Suddenly I look at her and she's not there. I look again, her absence defines her.

31. Benjamin, *Bonds of Love*, 21.

32. Ibid., 22.

33. Ibid., 26.

34. Elena Poniatowska recalls that during her own childhood she saw very little of her mother and father. She spent most of her time with nannies and governesses, who escorted her on perfunctory appearances before her parents. Later, as a mother herself, Poniatowska rejected this uninvolved style of parenting and strove to cultivate a close relationship with her children while also maintaining a professional life.

35. I was a child madly in love. A child who waited whole hours. A child like a faithful dog. A child caught between two doors, held up by her love. A child waiting at the top of the stairs. A child next to the window. Just seeing her made all my hours of waiting worth it. . . . I never pestered her, but alone I persisted in my illusions, I pierced her through, I spun her around, I dressed her up . . . We were two little girls adrift in Mexico. What a fragile lifeline held us.

36. She flutters around, her dress sweeping the floor, her eyes darting in all directions. / She walks slowly, unhearing, mama, her dress is pure wind.

37. Dear God, how pretty she is, how very pretty. I'll never be like her, ever. Even when she gets old, her face will be prettier than mine.

38. I sense her pulse beneath the cloth which doesn't protect her. How fragile the nape of her neck looks, a man could encircle it with one hand, encircle her whole neck with just one hand.

39. The staircase opens into a narrow passageway, and I walk under the tunnel; so many steps it takes to reach the light. Yellow lamps hang overhead, but I want the daylight.

40. In the essay on domestic servants which I have cited earlier, "Presentación al lector mexicano," Poniatowska describes her Mexican nanny Magdalena Castillo, clearly the model for Magda in *La "Flor de Lis."* She stresses the idea that Castillo unselfishly gave the best years of her youth to Elena and her sister, revealing both gratitude and guilt as the recipient of the other's sacrifice.

41. He remains aloof. He will always be that way, over on the other

shore. . . . I love papa when he avoids me, when his eyes are the green of insecurity and expectation; expectations that later I will find out are never fulfilled, because my father doesn't know the way, doesn't know how to get back into life.

42. Elena Poniatowska's father, Juan Evremont Poniatowski Sperry, was a paratrooper who, among other assignments, conducted reconnaissance missions behind German lines during World War II. When Poniatowska speaks of her father she mentions his secret heroism, his love for music, and a peculiar disengagement from everyday affairs that characterized his years in Mexico after the war.

43. I climb back into my foxhole and think about my loyal Patitas. I wonder where he is now? (Poniatowska, *De noche vienes*, 207).

44. Pratt, "Identity," 38.

45. Unlike the flowers of my great-grandmother, my grandmother, my mother, my aunt, mine will be paper flowers. But where will they bloom?

46. He's asking for something, but what? We're all willing to give it to him, but what does he want?

47. I cannot agree with Sara Poot Herrera's evaluation of Teufel as a *padre feminista*, called to liberate women and ultimately vindicated after his fall in the novel (*La 'Flor de lis'*). Cynthia Steele's identification of his "virulent *machismo*, manifested in the priest's abuse of his patriarchal authority to seduce his female followers," corresponds to my own view of the figure of Teufel in *La "Flor de Lis"* ("Other Within," 318).

48. Go to hell, get back into the mirror . . . ! Get away from me, sisters in sorrow, get away with your diamond-studded combs and your hair brushed one hundred strokes a day. I don't want my ideas tamed under your ivory-handled brushes and your inlaid heraldry.

49. My country is this stone bench where I sit watching the midday, my country is this sunlit slowness.

50. In Mexican literature only the novels of Nellie Campobello match Elena Poniatowska's achievement in treating the theme of mother-daughter relationships.

51. Rich, *Of Woman Born*, 224.

52. Ibid., my emphasis.

53. Ibid., 225.

54. Poniatowska, "Question Mark," 92.

BIBLIOGRAPHY

SELECTED WORKS BY ELENA PONIATOWSKA

Lilus Kikus. Mexico City: Colección Los Presentes, 1954.
"Melés y Teleo." *Revista Panoramas* 2 (1956): 135–299.
Palabras cruzadas; crónicas. Mexico City: Era, 1961.
Todo empezó el domingo. Mexico City: Fondo de Cultura Económica, 1963.
Los cuentos de Lilus Kikus. Mexico City: Universidad Veracruzana, 1967.
Hasta no verte Jesús mío. Mexico City: Era, 1969.
"Un libro que me fue dado." *Vida Literaria* (Mexico) 3 (1970): 3–4.
La noche de Tlatelolco: Testimonios de historia oral. Mexico City: Era, 1971.
"La borrega." "La procesión." "El recado." In *Cuentistas mexicanas siglo XX,* ed. Aurora M. Ocampo, 283–286. Mexico City: Universidad Nacional Autónoma de México, 1976.
"Prólogo." *El primer Primero de Mayo.* Mexico City: Centro de Estudios Históricos del Movimiento Obrero Mexicano, 1976.
Querido Diego, te abraza Quiela. Mexico City: Era, 1978.
"*Hasta no verte Jesús mío.*" *Vuelta* 24 (November 1978): 5–11.
De noche vienes. Mexico City: Grijalbo, 1979.
Gaby Brimmer and Elena Poniatowska. *Gaby Brimmer.* Mexico City: Grijalbo, 1979.
Fuerte es el silencio. Mexico City: Era, 1980.
La casa en la tierra. Photos by Mariana Yampolsky. Mexico City: INA-Fonapas, 1980.
Domingo siete. Mexico City: Ediciones Océano, 1982.

El último guajolote. Mexico City: Martín Casillas, 1982.
"Testimonios: Jesusa Palancares." *fem* 4.24 (1982): 33–35.
"Presentación al lector mexicano." *Se necesita muchacha.* Ana Gutié-
rrez, 7–86. Mexico City: Fondo de Cultura Económica, 1983.
"Testimonios de una escritora: Elena Poniatowska en micrófono." In
La sartén por el mango, ed. Patricia González and Eliana Ortega,
155–162. Río Piedras, Puerto Rico: Huracán, 1984.
Pablo O'Higgins. Mexico City: Fondo de Cultura Económica, 1985.
¡Ay vida, no me mereces! Mexico City: Joaquín Mortiz, 1986.
"Prólogo." In *Héctor García: México sin retoque.* Mexico City: Univ-
ersidad Nacional Autónoma de México, 1987.
Nada, nadie. Las voces del temblor. Mexico City: Era, 1988.
La "Flor de Lis." Mexico City: Era, 1988.
"Introduction." In *Cartucho and My Mother's Hands,* by Nellie Cam-
pobello, trans. Doris Meyer and Irene Matthews, vii–xiv. Austin:
University of Texas Press, 1988.
Juchitán de las mujeres. Photos by Graciela Iturbide. Mexico City: Edi-
ciones Toledo, 1989.
"Memoria e identidad: Algunas notas histórico-culturales." *Nuestra
América frente al V Centenario,* 124–139. Mexico City: Joaquín
Mortiz, 1989.
"La muerte de Jesusa Palancares." In *La historia en la literatura ibero-
americana,* ed. Raquel Chang-Rodríguez and Gabriella de Beer, 9–
22. Hanover, N.H.: Ediciones del Norte, 1989.
Todo México. Vol. 1. Mexico City: Editorial Diana, 1990.
Tinísima. Mexico City: Era, 1992.

TRANSLATIONS OF ELENA PONIATOWSKA INTO ENGLISH

Kolovakos, Gregory, and Ronald Christ, trans. "And Here's to You,
Jesusa." In *Lives on the Line: The Testimony of Contemporary Latin
American Authors,* ed. and introd. Doris Meyer, 137–155. Berke-
ley: University of California Press, 1988.
Lane, Helen R., trans. *Massacre in Mexico.* New York: Viking Press,
1975.
Miller, Beth, trans. "Love Story." *Latin American Literary Review* 13.26
(1985): 65–73.
Silver, Katherine, trans. *Dear Diego.* New York: Pantheon Books, 1986.
Steele, Cynthia, trans. "Bewitched By Words" and "Words That Be-
witch Us." Occasional Publications, Lectures I. Seattle. Romance
Languages and Literatures, University of Washington, 1989.

———. "A Question Mark Engraved on My Eyelids." In *The Writer on Her Work*, ed. Janet Sternberg, 82–96. New York: W. W. Norton, 1991.

———. "Slide in My Dark One, Between the Crosstie and the Whistle." In *Beyond the Border: A New Age in Latin American Women's Fiction*, ed. Nora Erro-Peralta and Caridad Silva-Núñez, 125–143. Pittsburgh: Cleis Press, 1991.

Wey, Nicolás, trans. "Literature and Women in Latin America." In *Women's Writing in Latin America*, ed. Sara Castro-Klarín, Sylvia Molloy, and Beatriz Sarlo, 80–87. Boulder: Westview Press, 1991.

White-House, Catherine S., trans. "The Night Visitor." In *Other Fires: Short Fiction by Latin American Women*, ed. Alberto Manguel, 125–145. New York: Clarkson N. Potter, 1986.

SECONDARY SOURCES

Criticism of the Works of Elena Poniatowska

Balboa Echeverría, Miriam. "Notas a una escritura testimonial: *Fuerte es el silencio* de Elena Poniatowska." *Discurso Literario* 5.2 (1988): 365–373.

Banchik-Rothschild, Roberto. "An Interview with Elena Poniatowska." *Third World Forum* (Davis, Calif.), February 1, 1988, 6,9.

Beer, Gabriella de. "La revolución en la narrativa de Campobello, Castellanos y Poniatowska." *Semana de Bellas Artes* (Mexico), January 28, 1981, 2–5.

Belejack, Barbara. "An Enormously Exciting Time: Interview." *Mexico Journal*, August 8, 1988, 3–4.

Berry, John. "Invention, Convention, and Autobiography in Elena Poniatowska's *Querido Diego, te abraza Quiela*." *Confluencia* 3.2 (1988): 47–56.

Bruce-Novoa, Juan. "Elena Poniatowska: The Feminist Origins of Commitment." *Women's Studies International Forum* 6.5 (1983): 509–516.

———. "Subverting the Dominant Text: Elena Poniatowska's *Querido Diego*." In *Knives and Angels: Women Writers in Latin America*, ed. Susan Bassnett, 115–131. London: Zed Books, 1990.

Capistrán, Miguel. "La transmutación literaria." *Vida Literaria* (Mexico) 3 (1970): 12–14.

Carballo, Emmanuel. "*Lilus Kikus*." *México en la Cultura*, November 7, 1954, 2.

———. "*Melés y Teleo*." *México en la Cultura*, July 15, 1956, 2.

Carmona, Krista Ratowski. "Entrevista a Elena Poniatowska." *Mester* 15.2 (1986): 37–42.

Cella, Susana Beatriz. "Autobiografía e historia de vida en *Hasta no verte Jesús mío* de Elena Poniatowska." *Literatura Mexicana* 2.1 (1991): 149–156.

Chevigny, Bell Gale. "The Transformation of Privilege in the Work of Elena Poniatowska." *Latin American Literary Review* 8.26 (1985): 49–62.

Christ, Ronald. "The Author as Editor." *Review* (Fall 1975): 78–79.

———. *"Los cuentos de Lilus Kikus."* *Recent Books in Mexico* 14.5 (1967): 5.

Davis, Lisa. "An Invitation to Understanding among Poor Women of the Americas. *The Color Purple* and *Hasta no verte Jesús mío.*" In Chevigny and Laguardia, eds., *Reinventing the Americas*, 224–241.

Dever, Susan. "Elena Poniatowska: La crítica de una mujer." In López-González, Malagamba, and Urrutia, eds., *Mujer y literatura*, 2: 107–112.

Donoso Pareja, Miguel. "La caducidad del realismo." *Vida Literaria* (Mexico) 3 (1970): 10–11.

Ferman, Claudia. "México en la posmodernidad: Textualización de la cultura popular urbana." *Nuevo Texto Crítico* 4.7 (1991): 157–167.

Flori, Mónica. "El mundo femenino de Marta Lynch y Elena Poniatowska." *Letras Femeninas* 9.2 (1983): 23–30.

———. "Visions of Women: Symbolic Physical Portrayal as Social Commentary in the Short Fiction of Elena Poniatowska." *Third Woman* 11.2 (1984): 77–83.

Foster, David William. "Latin American Documentary Narrative." *Publication of the Modern Language Association* 99.1 (January 1984): 41–55.

Fox-Lockert, Lucía. *Women Novelists in Spain and Spanish America.* Metuchen, N.J.: Scarecrow Press, 1979.

Franco, Jean. "Rewriting the Family: Contemporary Feminism's Revision of the Past." In *Plotting Women: Gender and Representation in Mexico*, 175–227. New York: Columbia University Press, 1989.

Friedman, Edward. "The Marginated Narrator: *Hasta no verte Jesús mío* and the Eloquence of Repression." In *The Antiheroine's Voice: Narrative Discourse and Transformations of the Picaresque*, 170–187. Columbia: University of Missouri Press, 1987.

Galindo, Carmen. "Vivir del milagro." *Vida Literaria* (Mexico) 3 (1970): 8–9.

García Flores, Margarita. "Entrevista a Elena Poniatowska." *Revista de la Universidad de México* 30.7 (1976): 25–30.

García Pinto, Magdalena. "Entrevista con Elena Poniatowska." In *Historias íntimas: Conversaciones con diez escritoras latinoamericanas*, 175–198. Hanover, N.H.: Ediciones del Norte, 1988.

———. *Women Writers of Latin America. Intimate Histories*, trans. Trudy Balch and Magdalena García Pinto. Austin: University of Texas Press, 1991.

García-Rodríguez, Antonia. "Female Feelings of Fragmentation in Rosario Ferré's *Papeles de Pandora* and Elena Poniatowska's *Hasta no verte Jesús mío*." *DAI* 49.7 (1989): 1816A.

García Serrano, M. Victoria. "Apropiación y transgresión en *Querido Diego, te abraza Quiela* de Elena Poniatowska." *Letras Femeninas* 17.1–2 (1991): 99–106.

Gautier, Marie-Lise Gazarian. "Elena Poniatowska." In *Interviews with Latin American Writers*, 200–216. Elmwood, Ill.: Dalkey Archive Press, 1989.

Gertel, Zunilda. "La mujer y su discurso: Conciencia y máscara." In *Cambio social en México visto por autores contemporáneos*, ed. José Anadón, 45–60. Notre Dame, Ind.: University of Notre Dame, 1984.

Gold, Janet M. "Elena Poniatowska: The Search for an Authentic Language." *Discurso Literario* 6.1 (1988): 181–191.

González-Lee, Teresa. "Jesusa Palancares, curandera espiritista o la patología de la pobreza." In López-González, Malagamba, and Urrutia, eds., *Mujer y literatura*, 2:93–97.

Hancock, Joel. "Elena Poniatowska's *Hasta no verte, Jesús mío*: The Remaking of the Image of Woman." *Hispania* 66.3 (1983): 353–359.

———. "*Hasta no verte, Jesús mío*: Una heroína liberada." *El Universal*, December 29, 1981, 22.

Jaén, Didier. "La neopicaresca en México: Elena Poniatowska y Luis Zapata." *Tinta* 1.5 (Spring 1987): 23–29.

Jörgensen, Beth E. "Elena Poniatowska." In *Spanish American Women Writers. A Bio-Bibliographical Sourcebook*, ed. Diane Marting, 472–482. Westport, Conn.: Greenwood Press, 1990.

———. "Elena Poniatowska." In *Escritoras hispanoamericanas*, ed. Diane Marting and Montserrat Ordóñez, 500–512. Bogotá: Siglo Veintiuno Editores, 1990.

———. "Framing Questions: The Role of the Editor in Elena Poniatowska's *La noche de Tlatelolco*." *Latin American Perspectives* 18.3 (Summer 1990): 80–90.

———. "La intertextualidad en *La noche de Tlatelolco* de Elena Poniatowska." *Hispanic Journal* 10.2 (1989): 81–93.

———. "Perspectivas femeninas en *Hasta no verte Jesús mío* y La *"Flor de Lis."* *Texto Crítico* 14.39 (1988): 110–123.

———. "Texto e ideología en la obra de Elena Poniatowska." Ph.D. diss., University of Wisconsin, 1986.

Kaminsky, Amy K. *Reading the Body Politic: Feminist Criticism and Latin American Women Writers.* Minneapolis: University of Minnesota Press, 1993.

Kerr, Lucille. "Gestures of Authorship: Lying to Tell the Truth in Elena Poniatowska's *Hasta no verte Jesús mío.*" *MLN* 106 (1991): 370–394.

Kostakowsky, Lya. "La entrevistadora entrevistada." *México en la Cultura*, May 26, 1957, 5, 11.

Kushigian, Julia. "Transgresión de la autobiografía y el *Bildungsroman* en *Hasta no verte Jesús mío.*" *Revista Iberoamericana* 140 (July–September 1987): 667–677.

Lagos-Pope, María Inés. "El testimonio creativo de *Hasta no verte Jesús mío.*" *Revista Iberoamericana* 150 (1990): 243–253.

Lemaître, Monique J. "Jesusa Palancares y la dialéctica de la emancipación femenina." *Hispamérica* 10.30 (December 1981): 131–135.

López Negrete, Cecilia. "Con Elena Poniatowska." *Vida Literaria* (Mexico) 3 (1970): 16–19.

Loustanau, Martha O. "Mexico's Contemporary Women Novelists." Ph.D. diss., University of New Mexico, 1973.

Méndez-Faith, Teresa. "Entrevista con Elena Poniatowska." *Inti* 15 (Spring 1982): 54–60.

———. "Translation of an Interview with Elena Poniatowska," trans. Elizabeth Heinicke. *Atlantis* 9.2 (Spring 1984): 70–75.

Menton, Seymour. "Sin embargo: La nueva cuentista femenina en México." *Tinta* 15 (1987): 35–37.

Miller, Beth. "Elena Poniatowska." In *Veinte y seis autoras del México actual,* 299–321. Mexico City: Costa-Amic.

———. "Interview with Elena Poniatowska." *Latin American Literary Review* 4.7 (1975): 73–78.

———. "Personas y personajes: Castellanos, Fuentes, Poniatowska y Sáinz." In *Mujeres en la literatura,* 65–75. Mexico City: Fleischer, 1978.

Monsiváis, Carlos. "'Mira, para que no comas olvido . . .' las precisiones de Elena Poniatowska." *La Cultura en México,* July 15, 1981, 2–4.

———. "A veinte años de *La noche de Tlatelolco.*" *Semanal,* supplement to *La Jornada,* October 13, 1991, 20–29.

Monterde, Francisco. "Cuadro vivo del pueblo." *Vida Literaria* (Mexico) 3 (1970): 5–7.

Ochoa Sandy, Gerardo. "De *Lilus Kikus* a *Luz y luna, las lunitas*." *Sábado*, suplemento de *Unomásuno*, February 11, 1989, 1, 3–4.

Pacheco, José Emilio. "Elena Poniatowska aporta, en sus incomparables crónicas, un espejo de la vida mexicana." *México en la Cultura*, October 30, 1961, 3.

Pérez Pisonero, Arturo. "Jesusa Palancares, esperpento femenino." In López-González, Malagamba, and Urrutia, eds., *Mujer y literatura*, 1: 221–229.

Pérez-Robles, Xiúhnel. "*La noche de Tlatelolco*." *Cuadernos Americanos* 177 (1971): 79–82.

Poot Herrera, Sara. "*La 'Flor de Lis'*, códice y huella de Elena Poniatowska." In López-González, Malagamba, and Urrutia, eds., *Mujer y literatura*, 2: 99–106.

Price, Greg. "Elena Poniatowska." In *Latin America: The Writer's Journey*, 233–243. London: Hamish Hamilton, 1990.

Reboreda, Aída. "Al terminar mi libro sobre Demetrio Vallejo haré una novela sobre mi mundo, la reacción: Poniatowska." *Unomásuno*, October 5, 1979, 17.

Resnick, Margery, and Isabelle de Courtivron. *Women Writers in Translation: An Annotated Bibliography 1945–1982*. New York: Garland Publishing, 1984.

Roses, Lorraine. "Entrevista con Elena Poniatowska." *Plaza* 5–6 (1981–1982): 51–64.

Saltz, Joanne. "*Hasta no verte Jesús mío*: Testimonio de una mujer." In López-González, Malagamba, and Urrutia, eds., *Mujer y literatura*, 1: 231–238.

Schaefer, Claudia. *Textured Lives: Women, Art, and Representation in Modern Mexico*. Tuscon: University of Arizona Press, 1992.

Scott, Nina M. "The Fragmented Narrative Voice of Elena Poniatowska." *Discurso Literario* 7.2 (1990): 411–420.

Smith, Richard Cándida. "'¿Quién quiere usted que sea bueno?'" *Oral History Review* 14 (1986): 73–82.

Starčević, Elizabeth D. "Breaking the Silence: Elena Poniatowska, a Writer in Transition." In *Literatures in Transition: The Many Voices of the Caribbean Area: A Symposium*, ed. Rose S. Minc, 63–68. Gaithersburg, Md.: Hispamérica, 1982.

———. "Elena Poniatowska: Witness for the People." In *Contemporary Women Authors of Latin America*, ed. Doris Meyer and Margarite Fernández Olmos, 72–77. Brooklyn: Brooklyn College Press, 1983.

Steele, Cynthia. "La creatividad y el deseo en *Querido Diego, te abraza Quiela*, de Elena Poniatowska." *Hispamérica* 41 (1985): 17–28.

———. "Entrevista: Elena Poniatowska." *Hispamérica* 53–54 (August–December 1989): 89–105.

———. "La mediación en las obras documentales de Elena Poniatowska." In López-González, Malagamba, and Urrutia, eds., *Mujer y literatura*, 1: 211–219.

———. *Politics, Gender, and the Mexican Novel, 1968–1988*. Austin: University of Texas Press, 1992.

———. "Testimonio y autor/idad en *Hasta no verte Jesús mío.*" *Revista de Crítica Literaria Latinoamericana* 18.36 (1992): 155–180.

Tatum, Charles M. "Elena Poniatowska's *Hasta no verte, Jesús mío* [Until I See You, Dear Jesus]." In *Latin American Women Writers: Yesterday and Today*, ed. Yvette E. Miller and Charles M. Tatum, 49–58. Pittsburgh: Review, 1977.

Torres, Juan Manuel. "Hasta el fin de la esperanza." *Vida Literaria* (Mexico) 3 (1970): 15.

Young, Rinda Rebeca Stowell. "Six Representative Women Novelists of Mexico, 1960–1969." Ph.D. diss., University of Illinois–Urbana Champaign, 1975.

Other Works Consulted

Abel, Elizabeth, Marianne Hirsch, and Elizabeth Langland, eds. *The Voyage In: Fictions of Female Development*. Hanover, N.H.: University Press of New England, 1983.

Avilés Fabila, René. *El gran solitario de palacio*. Buenos Aires: Compañía General Fabril Editora, 1971.

Bakhtin, Mikhail M. *The Dialogic Imagination*, trans. Caryl Emerson and Michael Holquist. Austin: University of Texas Press, 1981.

———. *Problems of Dostoevsky's Poetics*, trans. R.W. Rostel. Ann Arbor, Mich.: Ardis, 1973.

Bal, Mieke. *Narratology: Introduction to the Theory of Narrative*, trans. Christine van Boheemen. Toronto: University of Toronto Press, 1985.

Balam, Gilberto. *Tlatelolco: Reflexiones de un testigo*. Mexico City: Talleres Lenasa, 1969.

Barnet, Miguel. *Biografía de un cimarrón*. Barcelona: Ediciones Ariel, 1968.

———. "La novela testimonio: Socio-literatura." In Jara and Vidal, eds., *Testimonio*, 380–402.

Barnet, Miguel, and Esteban Montejo. *Autobiography of a Runaway Slave*, trans. Jocasta Innes. London: Bodley Head, 1966.

Benjamin, Jessica. *The Bonds of Love: Psychoanalysis, Feminism and the Problem of Domination*. New York: Pantheon, 1988.

Beverley, John. "The Margin at the Center: On *Testimonio* (Testimonial Literature)." *Modern Fiction Studies* 35.1 (Spring 1989): 1–28.

Blanco Moheno, Roberto. *Tlatelolco: Historia de una infamia*. Mexico City: Editorial Diana, 1969.

Borges, Jorge Luis. "La penúltima versión de la realidad." In *Discusión*. Buenos Aires: Emecé Editores, 1964.

Brushwood, John S. "Mexican Fiction in the Seventies: Author, Intellect, and Public." *Proceedings of the Comparative Literature Symposium* 10 (1978): 35–47.

———. *Mexico in Its Novel: A Nation's Search for Identity*. Austin: University of Texas Press, 1966.

Bruss, Elizabeth W. *Autobiographical Acts: The Changing Situation of a Literary Genre*. Baltimore: Johns Hopkins University Press, 1976.

Burgos, Elisabeth, and Rigoberta Menchú. *Me llamo Rigoberta Menchú y así me nació la conciencia*. Mexico City: Siglo Veintiuno Editores, 1985.

Cabrera Parra, José. *Díaz Ordaz y el '68*. Mexico City: Grijalbo, 1980.

Campos Lemus, Sócrates A. *El otoño de la Revolución (octubre)*. Mexico City: B. Costa-Amic, 1973.

Castillo, Debra A. *Talking Back: Toward a Latin American Feminist Literary Criticism*. Ithaca, N.Y.: Cornell University Press, 1992.

Chevigny, Bell Gale, and Gari Laguardia, eds. *Reinventing the Americas*. Cambridge: Cambridge University Press, 1986.

Chodorow, Nancy. *The Reproduction of Mothering: Psychoanalysis and the Sociology of Gender*. Berkeley: University of California Press, 1978.

Cohn, Dorrit. *Transparent Minds*. Princeton: Princeton University Press, 1978.

Cosío Villegas, Daniel, ed. *Historia general de México*. Mexico City: Colegio de México, 1976.

Culler, Jonathan. *On Deconstruction*. Ithaca, N.Y.: Cornell University Press, 1982.

de Lauretis, Teresa. *Alice Doesn't: Feminism, Semiotics, Cinema*. Bloomington: Indiana University Press, 1984.

Derrida, Jacques. "The Parergon," trans. Craig Owens. *October* 9 (1979): 3–40.

Eagleton, Terry. *Criticism and Ideology*. London: Verso Editions, 1978.

————. *Marxism and Literary Criticism*. Berkeley: University of California Press, 1976.

Foucault, Michel. *The Archaeology of Knowledge*, trans. A. M. Sheridan Smith. New York: Harper and Row, 1972.

————. "Intellectuals and Power." In *Language, Counter-memory, Practice*, ed. and trans. Donald F. Bouchard and Sherry Simon, 205–217. Ithaca, N.Y.: Cornell University Press, 1977.

Fuentes, Carlos. *Tiempo mexicano*. Mexico City: Joaquín Mortiz, 1971.

Genette, Gérard. *Narrative Discourse*, trans. Jane E. Lewin. Ithaca, N.Y.: Cornell University Press, 1980.

Gilligan, Carol. *In a Different Voice*. Cambridge: Harvard University Press, 1982.

Gluck, Sherna Berger, and Daphne Patai, eds. *Women's Words: Feminist Practice of Oral History*. New York: Routledge, 1991.

González de Alba, Luis. *Los días y los años*. Mexico City: Era, 1971.

Gyurko, Lanin A. "The Literary Response to Nonoalco-Tlatelolco." In *Contemporary Latin American Culture: Unity and Diversity*, ed. C. Gail Gunterman, 45–77. Tempe, Ariz.: Center for Latin American Studies, 1984.

Heilbrun, Carolyn G. *Reinventing Womanhood*. New York: W. W. Norton and Company, 1979.

————. *Toward a Recognition of Androgyny*. New York: Alfred A. Knopf, 1973.

Jara, René. "Prólogo: Testimonio y literatura." In Jara and Vidal, eds., *Testimonio*, 1–6.

Jara, René, and Hernán Vidal, eds. *Testimonio y literatura*. Minneapolis: Institute for the Study of Ideologies and Literatures, 1986.

Jelinek, Estelle C., ed. *Women's Autobiography: Essays in Criticism*. Bloomington: Indiana University Press, 1980.

Kristeva, Julia. *Desire in Language: A Semiotic Approach to Literature and Art*, ed. Leon S. Roudiez, trans. Thomas Gora, Alice Jardine, and Leon S. Roudiez. New York: Columbia University Press, 1980.

————. *El texto de la novela*, trans. Jordi Llovet. Barcelona: Editorial Lumen, 1974.

Langford, Walter M. *The Mexican Novel Comes of Age*. Notre Dame: University of Notre Dame Press, 1971.

Leacock, Eleanor, et al. *Women in Latin America*. Riverside, Calif.: Latin American Perspectives, 1979.

Lejeune, Philippe. *On Autobiography*, trans. Katherine Leary. Minneapolis: University of Minnesota Press, 1989.

León-Portilla, Miguel, ed. *Visión de los vencidos: Relaciones indígenas de la conquista*. Mexico City: Universidad Nacional Autónoma de México, 1959.

————, ed. *The Broken Spear*, trans. Lysander Kemp. Boston: Beacon Press, 1962.

Lerner, Gerda. *The Majority Finds Its Past*. New York: Oxford University Press, 1979.

López-González, Aralia, Amelia Malagamba, and Elena Urrutia, eds. *Mujer y literatura mexicana y chicana: Culturas en contacto*. 2 vols. Mexico City: Colegio de México, 1988, 1990.

Lorde, Audre. "The Master's Tools." *Sister/Outsider*, 110–113. Trumansburg, N.Y.: Crossing Press, 1984.

Mendoza, María Luisa. *Con El, conmigo, con nosotros tres*. Mexico City: Joaquín Mortiz, 1971.

Merrill, John C. *Handbook of the Foreign Press*. Baton Rouge: Louisiana State University Press, 1959.

Miller, Beth, ed. *Women in Hispanic Literature: Icons and Fallen Idols*. Berkeley: University of California Press, 1983.

Monsiváis, Carlos. *A ustedes les consta: Antología de la crónica en México*. Mexico City: Era, 1980.

————. *Días de guardar*. Mexico City: Era, 1970.

————. "Proyecto de periodización de historia cultural de México." *Texto Crítico* 1.2 (July–December 1975): 91–102.

Mora, Juan Miguel de. *Tlatelolco 1968: Por fin toda la verdad*. Mexico City: Editores Asociados, 1975.

Los narradores ante su público. Mexico City: Joaquín Mortiz, 1966.

Nebrija, Antonio de. *Gramática de la lengua castellana*, ed. Antonio Quilis. Madrid: Editora Nacional, 1980.

Partnoy, Alicia. *The Little School: Tales of Disappearance and Survival in Argentina*, trans. Alicia Partnoy, Lois Athey, and Saundra Braunstein. Pittsburgh: Cleis Press, 1986.

Patai, Daphne. "U.S. Academics and Third World Women: Is Ethical Research Possible?" In Gluck and Patai, eds., *Women's Words*, 137–153.

Paz, Octavio. *El laberinto de la soledad*. Mexico City: Fondo de Cultura Económica, 1959.

————. *Posdata*. Mexico City: Siglo Veintiuno Editores, 1970.

Portal, Marta. *Proceso narrativo de la Revolución Mexicana*. Madrid: Espasa-Calpe, 1980.

Prada Oropeza, Renato. "De lo testimonial al testimonio: Notas para un deslinde del discurso-testimonio." In Jara and Vidal, eds., *Testimonio*, 7–21.

Pratt, Minnie Bruce. "Identity: Skin Blood Heart." In Elly Bulkin, Minnie Bruce Pratt, and Barbara Smith, *Yours in Struggle: Three Feminist Perspectives on Anti-Semitism and Racism*, 11–63. New York: Long Haul Press, 1984.

Register, Cheri. "Literary Criticism." *Signs* 6.3 (Winter 1980): 268–282.

Revueltas, José. *México 68: Juventud y revolución*. Mexico City: Era, 1978.

Rich, Adrienne. *Of Woman Born: Motherhood as Experience and Institution*. New York: W. W. Norton, 1976.

Robinson, Lillian S. *Sex, Class and Culture*. Bloomington: Indiana University Press, 1978.

Ruffinelli, Jorge, et al. "Los escritores mexicanos ante su realidad." *Hispamérica* 11–12 (1975): 33–48.

Ruiz Castañeda, María del Carmen. "La mujer mexicana en el periodismo." *Filosofía y Letras* 30 (1956): 207–221.

Ruiz de Alarcón, Juan. *La verdad sospechosa*. Mexico City: Fondo de Cultura Económica, 1985.

Salas, Elizabeth. Soldaderas *in the Mexican Military: Myth and History*. Austin: University of Texas Press, 1990.

Secanella, María Petra. *El periodismo político en México*. Barcelona: Editorial Mitre, 1983.

Smith, Paul. *Discerning the Subject*. Minneapolis: University of Minnesota Press, 1988.

Smith, Sidonie. *A Poetics of Women's Autobiography*. Bloomington: Indiana University Press, 1987.

Sommers, Joseph. *After the Storm*. Albuquerque: University of New Mexico Press, 1968.

Spivak, Gayatri Chakravorty. "Can the Subaltern Speak?" In *Marxism and the Interpretation of Culture*, ed. Cary Nelson and Lawrence Grossberg, 271–313. Urbana: University of Illinois Press, 1988.

Spota, Luis. *La plaza*. 2d ed. Mexico City: Grijalbo, 1977.

Stacey, Judith. "Can There Be a Feminist Ethnography?" In Gluck and Patai, eds., *Women's Words*, 111–120.

Stanton, Domna. *The Female Autograph*. Chicago: University of Chicago Press, 1987.

Trías, Eugenio. *Teoría de las ideologías*. Barcelona: Ediciones Península, 1975.

Usigli, Rodolfo. *¡Buenos días, Señor Presidente!* Mexico City: Joaquín Mortiz, 1972.

———. *El gesticulador. Nueve dramaturgos hispanoamericanos*. Vol. 1, ed. Frank Dauster. Ottawa: Girol Books, 1979.

Viezzer, Moema, and Domitila Barrios de Chungara. *"Si me permiten hablar . . ." Testimonios de Domitila, una mujer de las minas de Bolivia*. 2d ed. Mexico City: Siglo Veintiuno Editores, 1978.

Weil, Simone. "Human Personality." In *Simone Weil: An Anthology*, ed. and trans. Sian Miles, 69–98. London: Virago Press, 1986.

Williams, Raymond. *Marxism and Literature*. Oxford: Oxford University Press, 1977.

Young, Dolly J. "Mexican Literary Reactions to Tlatelolco 1968." *Latin American Research Review* 20.2 (1985): 71–85.

INDEX